THE *Turning* OF THE *Tide*

Linda Herbert

Formatting and cover design by www.OpulentAgency.co.uk

ISBN: 9798364423368

Acknowledgements

My love and thanks go to all those who have helped me through my life, in my walk with Jesus.

In relation to writing this book I'd like to thank Joe Benjamin for all his love, input, guidance and wise advice he has given me along the way, helping me to 'stay on course'..... And, of course, his wife Josie - and her love in supporting Joe, and me through it all. Also my thanks for taking the book on its final journey to publication!

My thanks also go to Gill Bough for all her love, support and prayer throughout this, my first writing journey. And I especially want to thank her for her love and kindness in taking on the task of proofreading this book for me; which I so appreciate.

Table of Contents

Introduction

How It All Started

What on earth am I doing, writing a book? How did this happen?

I'm writing this late on the evening of 3 May 2016. I've not long finished watching a broadcast from Pastor Joe, of Eagle Mountain Church in Bridgwater, Somerset - speaking on Periscope. He said to those watching that there were books in some of us, and that there were people waiting to read those books so they could be helped and encouraged.

I recalled the time, when I was living in Surbiton, Surrey in the early eighties, when I was looking at a picture on my bedroom wall of the sea rolling in on the shore of a sandy beach and had the words "the turning of the tide" come into my head. As I looked at it I felt the Lord say to me that that's what He had done in my life! He had turned my life completely around and in another direction - just as happens with ocean waters on the shore twice a day!

What was the Lord referring to, and what was it that He had done in my life?

Around ten years previously, one night in January 1970, He had saved my life quite dramatically - when I was intent on finishing it.... You see He caused a lady (my landlady actually), who was stone deaf, to hear me in the garden where I had somehow got myself to - after swallowing goodness knows how many tablets, before attempting to gas myself. If she hadn't got help when she did - I certainly wouldn't be here sharing this with you.

That night in Surbiton, as I continued to look at the picture of the sea, after saying that's what He had done in my life - I felt the Lord go on to speak to me about writing a book - to share with others some of the things I had learned through it all. Initially I just laughed - and have needed since then to ask His forgiveness! It just seemed so 'not me'..... even though He gave me the title of the book - "The Turning of the Tide". And the title wasn't surprising really, in view of the thought I'd had looking at the picture earlier!

I have to tell you that I didn't ignore completely what happened that evening - although I came pretty close to it! I made one or two half hearted attempts to start writing something - by hand. Remember, it was the early '80's and I didn't even possess a typewriter of any sort - let alone a mobile phone, kindle, iPad or a tablet; they just didn't exist.... Not to mention the fact that I didn't really possess any writing skills as such either!

Fast forward through to May 2016, when the Lord spoke to me, or I should say, challenged me again about writing a book.

How could I ignore it, when the Lord spoke to me for a second time, about writing a book that would help others? And your next question might be to ask me: Why do I think I am qualified to write a book?

The truth is - I don't think that I am qualified, in fact it is just the opposite! BUT God is able and with Him all things are possible and I am still learning that I need to move out into the unknown and follow where He leads me - even if it scares me, and I end up 'doing it afraid' as a well known minister Joyce Meyer often shares.

The Outcome

Time to 'fast forward' again - and now it's 2022! I am just finishing the book in question and it's also time to complete the introduction (which I'm now in the process of doing) that I actually started in 2016.... Wow! It's certainly been a roller coaster ride!

As I've just been sharing with you - I pretty well ignored it when the Lord first spoke to me about this book, back in the early '80's! And I suppose I didn't really do all that much better the second time around. I did accept the challenge in 2016 but, once again, I never said anything to anyone for a long time afterwards..... In many ways I've felt a fair amount of shame at times at not trusting the Lord and getting on with it.

But, in fact, I'm realising now that, yet again, it has actually been the right timing. I wasn't really prepared before to have been able to write it. My Father has put a lot of work into me to prepare me and give me the ability to do so! Both in training me on the writing aspect - but, also and probably even more importantly, in bringing me to the point of being both emotionally and spiritually capable of doing so.

I was reminded the other day of the time many years ago, when a man of God said to me that the Lord would "send someone half-way across the world" - even if it was to only help one person. He knew what he was talking about - he'd just come back from a 3 day trip to Albania! When I remembered that, I found myself saying to the Lord that if this book was of help to just one person who reads it - then it was worth writing it.....

Actually, I have been helped so much personally in the writing and sharing of my life's journey with Jesus in this book - that I would have to say it's been worth it, full stop!

My Prayer

What is my prayer as you read and share my story? My prayer is that you will be challenged; that you will learn from the experiences that I've been through; but, most of all, that you will be encouraged in your own walk with Jesus. We serve a faithful God - He loves us, understands us, is extremely patient and will NEVER fail us.

Above all be so very blessed!

CHAPTER 1

God's Intervention

Chapter 1/1 God Steps In

Waking Up in Hospital

My eyes opened and I looked around, wondering where I was. Someone seemed to be hovering over me talking, but I couldn't make out what they were saying. Slowly it began to dawn on me that I was in hospital and I realised it was a nurse speaking to me. I think she was asking me what I had taken, but I couldn't understand why! I felt very dopey and was drifting in and out of consciousness. This feeling gradually subsided and, at the same time, flashbacks started coming to me and I began to remember what had happened before, and what should have been the end of it all.

But God.... whatever situation we might find ourselves in, whether we believe in Him or not, the fact is He is ALWAYS there with us and can turn a situation completely around. This is especially the case when we don't feel that He is there - and He was certainly there with me that night, as you will see as you read on!

My hand, my left one I think, was hurting and, as I lifted it up to look at it, there appeared to be what looked like the outline of a cross on it marked in red. I realised later that it had got caught in the brambles in the garden, and the red actually was blood where it had got scratched. ***It definitely reminded me of Jesus, but I didn't get any further than that at that point.***

I couldn't tell the nurse what I'd taken, as I didn't really understand what she meant by the question! Added to which I couldn't actually remember taking anything. I think I spent most of that first night just drifting in and out of consciousness. I certainly wasn't aware, until they told me - next day I think, that they'd actually pumped out my stomach prior to my coming round and them talking to me. I also found out next day that I was in Homerton Hospital in Hackney - not really a surprise as it was situated more or less at the end of the road where I lived.

As I remained awake for longer periods of time, and my mind began to 'settle' somewhat, I began to slowly piece together what had happened to me that night. I had been to the Monday night church group I usually attended, taken by Angela, the Vicar's wife, at the local Anglican Church. All I can remember is sharing with them that I was finding things tough, but I believed that God would see me through. I did not tell them the bit about me buying as many tablets as I could during the day, and the plan to take them all later that night when I went back to my flat!

As I write this now, it makes me realise how easy it is to fool those around us; and ourselves as well.... Looking back, it never seemed to occur to me that, although I might have convinced the other people in the group, there was no way I could have convinced God. He looks on our heart and He knew exactly what I intended to do that night. Something that I would need to ask His forgiveness for at a later date, but didn't come into the equation at that point.

When I got home from the group, I proceeded with my plan, if you could call it a plan! It was cold so I filled a hot water bottle, and I put a blanket on the floor in front of the oven because the floor was cold. I wedged the table under the door handle so it would be hard to open and, at some stage, I must have written down my sister's details in Kent but I can't remember doing that at all. Then I set out to swallow as many of the tablets I could get down me, mostly Anadin I think..... I do remember that at one stage, due to the amount of water I was having to use to swill the tablets down, that a load of water came back up. I've never been very keen on taking tablets since that time!

At some stage, I believe it was after taking the tablets and before I turned the gas on, I took a long look into my eyes in the mirror and realised they portrayed something pretty awful..... Something that was going to play an important part at a later date and that the Lord was going to use in a specific way.

It was after this that I turned the gas on and settled down on the blanket I'd put in front of the oven. I'm guessing that my mind was basically numb by the time I got to this point and I was past thinking or feeling anything and just wanted it to be over. After that I don't remember anything at all until I started 'coming to' in hospital.

I know now that God had definitely stepped into the situation and I have thanked Him many times for His love in doing so.

Moving to the Psychiatric Wing

They didn't keep me in the Ward where I woke up, for very long. I presume I was taken into A &E initially before being taken to that first Ward, where I think I probably spent the rest of that day and the first night..... not that I remembered very much about it afterwards. Then I was moved to the Psychiatric Wing, where I stayed until I was discharged.

All I remember about going to the Psychiatric Ward was being taken there and into the office and spoken to, I presume by the Ward Sister, but I don't know what was said to me - and I don't think that's just that it was a long time ago, although it's over fifty years.... I don't think I took in very much of what was said to me at the time! I just remember still feeling dazed, thinking there was a strange atmosphere and, to be honest wondering, whether once I was in the Psychiatric Ward, I'd ever get out again.

After the session in the office I was taken along to the bed that I had been allocated to and the main thing I remember about it was that it was situated in the corner. This meant I wasn't bang in the middle with both sides of the bed on view to the rest of the

Ward - ***something I was thankful to the Lord for - although at that stage I wasn't conscious of still talking to Him....*** Actually I think it was the first bed on the right going into what was the 'female' section of the Ward because it was a mixed Ward, with men in one half and women in the other. There was a wardrobe and a bedside cabinet for me to put my possessions in - the only thing was..... I hadn't got anything to put in them, because of the circumstances that I'd come in under. Thinking about it, I must presumably have had on the clothes I was wearing when I'd made the suicide attempt....

There were several other occupants but I don't think all the beds were taken. I think it might well have been the afternoon by the time I got as far as being given a bed as I don't remember much else about the day..... only that I was very tired! I can only presume we had something to eat and drink at some stage during the late afternoon and evening.

What I do remember, vividly, was the actual bedtime that first night on the Ward. There was an older lady across on the other side and further along, in a sort of diagonal direction. I saw that she'd got herself ready for bed and looked as though she might be about to get into the bed and settle down. But, instead of that, she put both hands up and was 'yanking' at her hair, and the next minute the hair, which in fact was a wig, was in her hands and she was standing there with a completely bald head grinning at me! I didn't know whether to laugh or cry or possibly even scream..... it was such a shock, and I felt as though I had become the inmate of a mad house - which I suppose, in some respects, was in actual fact the case.

As you can probably guess, those first few days in the Ward were all a bit of a blur..... although some of the things that happened made their mark! There was one morning in particular I remember, because of the reaction it brought about in me, and I've always believed that was why the Lord allowed it to happen. One of the other female patients who was possibly around my age or slightly older, I was 26 at the time, became very disturbed. She started shouting and then got on to her bed and did her utmost to try and force a way out of the window. We were on the first or second floor, I'm not sure which, but it would have probably been fatal if she'd been successful and jumped. There were bars at the window so, although the window itself was partly open, there was no way she could have got out. Those of us who were nearby, I was almost opposite on the other side of the room, rushed across to restrain her and persuade her down off the bed. The nursing staff were very speedy at getting there and soon she'd been given something to calm her down.

It was some time before I found myself calm again! It had been quite upsetting to watch and to have been involved in.... I should explain that, ever since I had arrived in the hospital and had been capable of thinking about what had happened to me, I had become more and more determined that, somehow, I was going to get out and finish off what I'd started. I'd even thought further ahead that, if I couldn't escape from the hospital, I'd wait until I was at a stage of having slightly more freedom - and complete my mission then.

A Change in Direction

'But God' - two such amazing words, with such power - He had other plans for me!

When that lady tried to get through the window, the Lord did something inside of me, in my spirit. I felt the first 'spark' of a desire that I might want to stay alive, rather than to finish off what I'd started. It was a slow process before I got to the point where I definitely knew that never again would I attempt to take my life, but I'd taken the first step. I didn't realise that I'd be taking another one quite soon after that!

The next step taken was the afternoon that Angela, the Vicar's wife, whom I mentioned earlier, came to see me on the Ward. She told me how her heart had sunk when she heard which Ward I was on, because she knew it was the Psychiatric Ward. Looking back I realise that she found that visit to me quite difficult but, bless her, she still came.

It was definitely the Lord Who brought her, as she had the 'key' to the next step.... She shared with me from Isaiah about God's love for me. It was the verse in Isaiah 43:4 where the Lord says ".....you are precious in my sight.... and I love you." It so resonated in my spirit and, again, I had that 'spark' of a desire that I might want to stay alive!!

I don't particularly remember talking with her about it, but I think that's when we discussed me going and staying with her and the family for a while, when I was allowed to leave hospital.

It didn't happen 'overnight' but, I don't remember pursuing any more specific thoughts about continuing to complete, at some stage, the attempt I'd made to leave this world prematurely. ***It really wasn't the Lord's timing for me to go home*** so, if it had been successful, it would definitely have been premature.

The episode where I had helped the other lady in the Ward, plus Angela talking to me about the Lord's love for me and the wording of that verse in Isaiah, with the emphasis that I was 'precious' to the Lord - all added up to a change in the direction I was heading in.... Praise the Lord!

Life On the Ward

The days on the Ward sometimes seemed to drag but, looking back now, I don't really know how long they kept me there at the hospital. I did have some other visitors, beside Angela, who came in to see me. My eldest sister Jill, the one who I had left the details of for my landlady to let her know what had happened, came up from Kent. I think she possibly came prior to Angela's visit because I remember her saying to me that I'd 'be alright' - I 'still had my religion'..... only the trouble was, at that point, I knew that I hadn't! From my point of view I didn't feel I had anything - which is why I think she came before Angela had talked with me!

In actual fact, at that point I didn't feel that I had anything that worked in my life regarding a relationship with God.

A dear friend by the name of Doreen came to see me one afternoon, she is no longer here as she went home to be with the Lord quite a number of years ago now. Again, my memory of her visit was of her sitting holding my hand and I suppose I must have talked to her, but I have no idea what about or for how long!

The Plan going Forward

As I said earlier, I don't know how long they kept me in the hospital. The plan seemed to be that I should see some sort of consultant psychiatrist - someone in the London area, but who wasn't in the hospital, because I remember going to his consulting 'rooms' elsewhere. During the time I was waiting to see him, Angela and her husband John, who was the vicar at the local Anglican Church in Homerton, kindly invited me to stay with them; the next part of the plan! After that, in due course, once I'd been given some sort of an assessment by the psychiatrist, I would go down to stay with my sister in Southborough, Tunbridge Wells in Kent. At that stage my family would decide what was best for me to do after that.....

I wasn't in a place in my thinking at that stage for me to remember that my Heavenly Father would have already had it all planned out as to what was best for me. I hadn't really got past the stage where it was still a 'success' from my point of view, to be able to get through the current day - never mind sorting out how to get through the following days!

Again, I don't remember much about my visit to the psychiatrist, all a bit of a blur, or what his assessment was really. I think he came to the conclusion I'd started to move forward from what had happened but that, initially, it would be better for me not to be on my own! Whilst at my sister's, she and my parents agreed that, more long term, it would be best if my parents came over from Germany (they were based in Düsseldorf where my father was part of the British Army Fire Service) and take me back to live with them.

I didn't realise it then, but I can see now how it was all part of Father's plan for me.

Staying with Angela and Family

You can probably imagine how wonderful I found it moving into the vicarage with Angela and the family. Such a transformation after being on the Psychiatric Ward! I remember that one of the things I did whilst I was there, and something that so helped my mental state, was taking Angela's youngest child to a local park to play on the swings. I didn't realise it at the time, but looking back, I now understand how much she must have trusted the Lord to let me do that!

My friend Wendy came to visit me, but again, I don't really remember very much of what we talked about, although I realise it must have been hard for her to know what to say, etc. I do remember saying to her at one point that the mornings were hard when I first woke up - there'd be a few moments and then it all came flooding back as to what had happened.... and that, momentarily, I'd wish that I hadn't woken up!

I said earlier that it was a slow process before I got to the point where I definitely knew that never again would I attempt to take my life. One of the things that helped was having a long talk with John and him extracting a promise from me that, if ever I did feel suicidal in the future, that I would ring him before I did anything. He said he'd come and meet me wherever I was at that time, and we could talk. Having made that promise I knew that it would never get further than a 'thought'. At a later stage in my life I did ask the Lord to wipe it out of my mind!

Going to Kent with My Sister

My sister came back up to London and came with me on my visit to the Psychiatrist. Once again I can't remember particularly what he said to me, but I think my impression was mainly that he didn't really seem to know or understand what I was going through! An old cliche I suppose of someone who'd tried what I had..... However, he did release me, and I wasn't tied down to going back for a check up at any time! Again something that looking back on, I do so thank the Lord for.

After that I said a grateful goodbye to John and Angela and I headed off to Kent, in the care of my sister.... and a period of time which was, in many ways more difficult to get through. Some of the reason for this was, I think, the fact that I felt very much in limbo. A time of waiting, but not really knowing what exactly I was meant to be waiting for!

My parents rang from Germany and we spoke for the first time since it had all happened. I didn't really know what to say, but tried to say how sorry I was for all the worry I'd put them through! They didn't know what to say either, and ended up saying even less than I had.... We weren't a family that opened up to one another and talked things through particularly and, to be honest, I don't ever remember having an in depth conversation about it, or anything near to it, in any of the remaining years to come. Or, in fact, with any of my family, although I wouldn't want to blame them in any way, as I would imagine for the most part that I probably wasn't particularly willing to! They said they would come over to collect me from my sister in due course. They were staying with my Aunt Elsie, Dad's sister who lived not far away, whilst they were here in England.

I have no recollection of how long I was staying with my sister prior to my parents coming, although looking back it seemed quite a long time! As I said earlier, I felt very much in limbo, with the days being much the same and almost running into each other.... I'd stayed there many times before so it was all familiar, but all rather aimless!

I have found through the years that there are some situations that we find ourselves in that can seem as though they're going to last forever! But I have also realised that, sometimes it's in those same situations, that I have learned things in my walk and relationship with Jesus that I would never have learned otherwise. And I also have to acknowledge that I don't always recognise that to be the case until later. I suppose that what I'm really trying to say is - don't rush to discount the circumstances you're in. They are the very circumstances that Father has planned for you - even when it doesn't feel as though they are!

Chapter 1/2 The Lord's Dealings in Dusseldorf

Waiting for the Next Step

As I explained at the end of the first section of this chapter, I have no real recollection of how long I was staying at my sister's in Kent - it just seemed a long time! Thinking about it now, I guess it must have been difficult for my sister, and I don't think she really knew what to do with me! But I'm so glad that the Lord did!!

What I do remember is going out to do things like shopping etc - which got me out of the house, gave me some exercise and gave me something to do. None of which I was particularly interested in doing, I might add. Alongside the days going out, were the days in the house when I didn't know what to do with myself!

There are two occasions in particular that I remember from that initial period of waiting at my sister's home. The first arose from the difficulty I found in concentrating on anything for very long - and this was especially so in relation to reading. I found this extended into the realm of reading my Bible and I seemed unable to spend very long reading any part of it at all. And whatever I did read, I found that I couldn't remember any of it and hadn't got a clue what I had been reading. All somewhat disconcerting.....

But I also had with me a devotional book called "Edges of His Ways" by a lady called Amy Carmichael, who had been a missionary working with, and rescuing children in southern India. I had come across her books prior to going to train as a teacher and had this particular book with me when I went to my sister's, as well as my Bible. I felt it was so much the provision of the Lord as I found I could cope with reading the one, possibly two verses from the Bible that each daily devotion was based on. And, because the 'snippet' that Amy C shared with it was short, encouraging and often challenging as well - I was able somehow to take it in.

Once again the Lord was a step ahead of me, which I find is so often the case - though I do wish that I had learned that earlier in my life! I have realised and learned that, as the Lord takes me along in a certain direction that He has planned out - He has so often gone ahead of me and arranged things that only He could know I would need. This situation was a classic example of it, in the way He had made sure that I had that book by Amy Carmichael with me. I have no recollection of going back to the flat, let alone of getting that book - and yet it would play a vital part in the days to come!

I used that book for a very long time afterwards and, through it, the Lord began to slowly build up the crumbled walls of my faith. I remember in particular one morning when the reading was based on 1 John 1:9 "If we confess our sins, he is faithful and just to forgive us our sins, and to cleanse us from all unrighteousness." KJV. I'm pretty sure that I had read this verse before but, that morning, it was as though I was seeing it for the first time.

One of the many things I found really difficult after I came out of hospital, and began to try and get some semblance of my life together again and go forward, was forgiving myself for what I had done. When I read that verse and what Amy C said (which I have to be honest and say I can't remember now what it was) the Lord spoke to me about the importance of two things. The first - that if I asked Him to forgive me and I accepted His forgiveness, He would cleanse me from what I had attempted to do.

The second - that it was vital that, having accepted His forgiveness, I also needed to forgive myself for what I had done and allow the Lord to free me from the guilt of it. I realised, even in those early days, that if I didn't do that - I would live the rest of my life with that guilt hanging over me and wouldn't be free from it. Through the years, I've always been so grateful to the Lord for revealing that to me, helping me to see it and, through His Holy Spirit, helping me to act on it. As you can imagine, it didn't come very easily!

Actually I really feel that this lesson, which the Holy Spirit taught me (always remember that John tells us in his Gospel that the Holy Spirit is our teacher John 14:26) is one which is so important for us all to learn. It's so much easier to remain in guilt over things we have done - both big and small, than to turn to the Lord and get it sorted. And that's when the enemy dances with glee and brings up as many of his sly lies as he can to keep us in turmoil (guilt) about it; when we should be walking in peace with Jesus.

The second occasion that arose - and at this stage I'm not sure when it was, although I think it was quite early on after I got to my sister's.... I can remember sitting and looking at the clock in the room where I was, and thinking how incredibly slowly the time was passing by. I began to wonder how on earth I was going to cope with all the time I had on my hands and what I could do to survive the days and weeks ahead with no knowledge of what was going to happen!

Then I remembered from somewhere - looking back I realise that it must have been the Holy Spirit that brought it to mind - "My times are in thy hand...." Psalm 31:15 KJV. Every moment of every day is held in my Father's hands and all I need to concentrate on is the day that I am currently in!

However, at that stage I couldn't really concentrate on a 'whole' day - I found that I would look at the clock, and ask the Lord to help me get through the next hour.... and then the next, and so on through the day. After all, each day is made up of hours - so if I asked for help to get through each hour, the hours would eventually, together make up a whole day!

Through the years since then, and there have been a lot of them, I have so often appreciated the Holy Spirit showing and teaching me that lesson! In fact, I gradually came to realise that really it was the only way to live my life - to concentrate on 'today' and all the Lord wanted me to do and learn in it. I have found especially that, when the enemy comes with lies to wind me up over what's going to happen on any future day that might be coming - I can remind him that I am living in today, and Jesus might come back before any other days might get here! Try it -

you'll find it really works!!

My Parents Arrive in Kent

I don't want to labour the point, but I really do not have any recollection as to how long I stayed at my sister's while I waited for my parents to come over from Düsseldorf to collect me. Or, for that matter how long they were here for, before taking me back with them. Thinking about it, I presumably must have gone back at some point to where I was living in Homerton, to clear out my things. I couldn't have left my possessions there, as I wouldn't be going back to live there again.

I guess my sister would have taken me to pick them up, prior to going down to Kent. I have a complete 'blank' about doing that..... Whether my mind has chosen to block some things out completely, I just don't know - but there does seem to be some things that just seem to have 'gone'!

On My Way to Germany

No matter how long, or short for that matter, the time was before I was on the way with my parents - we eventually boarded the ferry to head across the channel, and then drive through to Düsseldorf. At least it wasn't completely new territory, as I'd visited them there before - so had some idea of what I was heading for.....

But, and it was a big BUT..... what was I heading towards? And what on earth was I going to do with myself - living back at my parents home at the age of 26 - and in a foreign country to boot? My father would be out at work - Fire Officer at the Army Base of Düsseldorf, where we lived in an Army quarter (house). My mother didn't go out to work and, fortunately we got on well together - but she was now landed with her youngest daughter living at home again, after being completely independent for many years! Not an easy task for her, for either of us really - especially in the circumstances that had brought it about!

After all that had happened, plus having had more contact through the years with people experiencing problems with their mental health - I realise by this stage I had, to a certain extent shut down parts of my thinking. I won't go as far as saying I'd shut God out and I've already shared moments when I quite obviously let Him in but, by and large, He didn't have too much space in my thinking during this time. You'll see this changed as time went by, but at this point it remained relatively the same!

Settling Down In Düsseldorf

At least there was plenty of space in my parents' house so we weren't on top of each other all the time, and I had my own room etc. But what to do with myself? I'd always loved reading but at this point in time I wasn't really able to concentrate sufficiently. Mum and I went into town on the bus and 'browsed'! Unfortunately I'd never been one for drifting round shops particularly - and it still isn't a popular choice of mine. It was kind of her to make the effort and I appreciated it, but I wasn't able to cope with too many trips....

One of the things I did do quite a lot of, especially initially, was 'jigsaws'. Yes, you heard me correctly - I did say jigsaws. I think maybe there were one or two in the house and then, as I found them helpful, I bought more - in particular the harder, more difficult ones to complete as they were a challenge. I found that I could sit working on a jigsaw with the radio or records playing (before the days of cd's!) - mainly classical music I believe, and I could 'switch off' from all that had happened! I suppose it was my way of escape from the reality of what life was like for me at that moment.

Another thing I started doing was going for walks in the area where my parents were living - weather permitting. I'm not sure of the date when we arrived out in Düsseldorf, especially as I wasn't sure how long I was in Kent with my sister - but I guess it was probably some time in March when we got there. There was plenty of countryside to explore as we weren't in town but a fair way out because of it being the British Army Base.

I guess it was on those walks that I began tentatively to start talking to the Lord again and slowly start to rebuild a relationship with Him. There was an Army Garrison Church on the Base that I must have found out about at some stage, because in due course I started going when I was able to on a Sunday morning. From memory there weren't very many lively clergy taking the services, although there seemed quite a change over of people. I also don't really remember making much contact with other people in the congregation.

I realise now that by just going regularly and being a part of a service that was being held to glorify God, stirred up and watered the seeds in my spirit. Seeds that, to be honest I thought at one point had all died off! Not that long after I came back to England, later in the year, I realised that going out to Germany - completely away from virtually all Christian contact / fellowship, was one of the best things the Lord could have done for me!! From a faith point of view I was completely on my own apart from the Lord - and I had to get on and find a new relationship with Him that worked, ***with no one else around to lean on!***

Later in the year, when I was back and settled into a job in England - my friend Wendy shared with me how my letters to her and Doreen, her flat mate, had challenged them both. She said that, ***as I shared with them they realised my relationship with the Lord was growing and strengthening and it challenged them and made them hungry to go deeper with the Lord themselves. I was completely unaware of this at the time but, thinking about it all these years later, it makes me realise how Father uses us to grow His Kingdom without us, very often, even being aware of it.***

Doing Something Positive Again

As time went by and I began to feel stronger as the Lord was healing me both physically and mentally, I found I wanted to be doing more than jigsaws, shopping expeditions and walking! I have to say though, that I had grown to love my walks out in the country with the Lord and not only talked with Him but had begun singing praise and worship songs as well. The song that has particularly stayed in my spirit since that time is the old hymn "Great is Thy Faithfulness". I used to sing this as loud as I could - and right up to the present day I find it so moving because of the association with all the Lord did in my life during that year of 1970.

A job vacancy came up at the NAAFI shop, on the Army Base, which wasn't very far from where I was living with my parents and meant I could walk to work. Realistically I think it was probably part-time as I don't think I would have been quite ready at that point to have worked full-time. It helped me to get back into some sort of a routine and gave me some feeling of being a bit more independent. Mainly I think it was stacking shelves etc, something I could have done in pretty well any supermarket in England! A lot of the items I was stacking were tins. Tins of pretty well anything there was going - but mainly tins of various foods.

It was the tins that turned out to be my 'down fall'..... I started itching and coming out in rashes all over the place, including the places where I had metal hooks on my bra - which turned out to be the most uncomfortable! I ended up having to see the doctor and found that I was reacting to the metal in the tins I was handling, and it had also caused a reaction to the metal hooks of my bra. It was somewhat frustrating, to say the least of it..... and in the end my time of working at the NAAFI had to come to an end.

One of the interesting things that resulted from my time there was thinking of the future more long term. There were teachers living on the base, because of being needed in the Army school presumably.... and at least one of them used to have the Times Educational Supplement, as it was called then (I think it might simply be known now as Tes), delivered with the other papers from England. I noticed it one day and found myself browsing through the teaching posts being advertised!

I think, if I'm honest, that I'd not given much thought, if any, since everything had happened, to the idea of going back into teaching again at a later date....

I never realised at the time that it was another 'God moment' - that it was the first step that the Lord put in place concerning doing just that. In fact I believe it was probably the very reason He had me working in the NAAFI to 'kick start' things! So often these apparently 'little' things happen and we never fully realise until later, and even sometimes not at all, just how important they are - and what a big part they play in God's scheme for our lives.

Another Step On the Way to Recovery

So once again I had time on my hands, but really needed to be active. As you can possibly guess - the Lord already had it safely in His hands. Next door to the house where I was staying with my parents, a young Welsh couple lived with, I think, three children. I think I remember the husband being a teacher - his wife I know ran a playgroup come nursery for the children of the soldiers and their wives. I'd come to know her quite well since I'd been there and it 'just happened', although I don't believe there are any coincidences with God, that she needed someone else to help her!

I went with her every morning to help with the children she looked after and I think, if I've remembered correctly that it was just the mornings so, although it was every day, they were half days and I coped ok with that. If you remember, one of the things I shared that helped when I stayed with Angela, was taking her youngest child to the park. Again, I found spending time with the children at the playgroup / nursery was tremendously beneficial to my mental health in recovering from the suicide attempt. I was so grateful to the Lord at the time, and still am, that He arranged that for me and the healing that came out of it.

Heading Back to England

I am not sure of all the details, but I believe my father applied to return to England because of family circumstances. The 'family circumstances' basically being 'me' - and in due course he was posted to a place called Kineton in the Midlands, where there was an Army ammunition depot. I was included in the move as my parents had asked me to continue to live at home with them initially when we returned to England and look for a job in that area. As you can imagine I wasn't really in a position to disagree.... so that became the plan we were moving towards as a family.

BUT - before I go any further in recounting what happened when I returned to England with my parents, I think I need to share some of the background that took me to the place where I needed God to step into my life in the powerful way that He did. I know that if He hadn't - there's no way that I would be here sharing this with you.

I do believe that one of the ways that helps in coming out of / recovering from any traumatic situation is the opportunity to be involved in some activity whereby you are moving out to others around you. This is especially so if the involvement is connected with something you've been involved in prior to the trauma. For me, I had spent quite a lot of time working with children in the past so, to now be doing this again gave me not only a sense of usefulness but also of normality - and of course it helped me get my mind off myself and the circumstances I found myself in. God is so, so good and always knows exactly what you need - even if you don't at first always recognise it for yourself.

CHAPTER 2

Encounters With God Bringing Change

Chapter 2/1 How Did it All Begin?

My Family Background

Well, I don't know that I need to tell you that I come from an Army family, as I've said earlier that my Father was in the Army Fire Service. That wasn't always the case, as he originally was apprenticed (I believe he left school at 14) to, and then worked for a printing firm in Tonbridge, Kent. However, as with so many others, when the Second World War broke out in 1939, he was drafted into the army at the age of 28. By then he was married with three children, and a fourth was added when I was born in 1944.

After the war he stayed in the army, and by then there were five of us - my youngest brother having been born in Austria just before we all returned to England in 1948. Our family were living in Tonbridge in Kent, although Dad was based in the North of England so we didn't see a great deal of him. My grandmother and great aunt also lived with us during that time, so it was a full house!

Dad stayed in the Army Fire Service for the remainder of his working life so, if you have any knowledge of army life, you'll know that I spent a great deal of my childhood on the move! I lived in a variety of places and frequented quite a few schools. I believe with some children this would have helped them to become more extrovert and capable of getting on with people.

Unfortunately, this wasn't the case with me and, although I didn't become an introvert, I did find it difficult at times to mix with other children and make proper friends. I didn't have a great deal of confidence, either in myself or in the strength of any friendship lasting - or whether I was actually liked or not....

Early Interest in God

I was seven and attending a Junior School, when we set off to join my Dad in Kuala Lumper, Malaya in 1952. He had gone ahead, which left my mother to trail five children on a four week sea voyage on her own. Unfortunately it was the army's way of doing things!

During the time we were in Tonbridge, I joined an organisation known as Juno's at the local parish church. Juno's was the younger section, the infants if it's easier to understand, of Pathfinders. I'm not sure of how long I was a Juno but I do remember something that happened to me during that time. I believe I made a tentative commitment to Jesus. I say 'tentative' as, all I remember really, was crossing my arm across my stomach and saying (and I'm not even very sure of what words I used) that I wanted to commit to following Jesus.

That was all I can recall about the occasion, but I believe it was the first footfall towards a lifelong relationship with Jesus! How wonderful to realise that our Heavenly Father hears and honours what happens in our hearts - even at the young age of seven! He knows whether you mean what you say and He nurtures you going forward.... and I know that He has been nurturing me every step of the way since, even, and maybe especially, through the times when I've not been aware of it.

Kuala Lumpur, Malaya

We had two years out in Malaya, the normal length of an army posting, and were based in Kuala Lumper. We were in a flat in town initially whilst waiting for an army quarter further out of town to become available. I attended the army school and was picked up every morning by an army truck and transported to school, in much the same way as the school buses do today. I was, of course, returned home at the end of the day in the same way! I'd put on weight when we moved to Malaya and one of my memories of travelling on the truck to school, is having rhymes about me being fat, sung to me on the journey. Not a great thing to build up self-esteem!

I went each day on my own as my younger brother hadn't reached school age by then, and my two sisters were too old for the army school which was the equivalent of our junior schools in England. Jill and Maureen, my two older sisters, went to a boarding school up country in the Cameron Highlands. My eldest brother had left school before we went out to Malaya, and he had got himself a job in the town of Kuala Lumper.

We were in Malaya at the time of the Emergency - which is why the British Army was out there. This meant that travelling any distance could be dangerous and meant that when my sisters travelled to the Cameron Highlands to go to school - they went under armed escort. I can remember us going up there to spend a holiday and being quite excited at travelling under escort!

I don't recall going to church much whilst being out in Malaya - I wasn't really of an age when I could go off on my own. Actually I did join the Brownies whilst we were there and I would imagine we might have attended the odd service as a group, but nothing has stayed in my memory at all. The Queen's coronation took place in June 1953 and I remember all the celebrations that went on and I guess we more than likely went to a church service at that time. With Dad being part of the army I'm sure he would have been involved in all that was going on.

Back to Life in England

We returned to England in July 1954. I was ten by that stage and, young as I was, I still remember how cold it was when the time came to get off the airplane. Yes, we flew home! No long sea journey this time although, compared to current flying times in the year 2022, it took a long time. In 2019 I flew back from Australia and the stage between Singapore and England took us 13 hours. The same distance back in 1954, took us five days!

Once again, at first there were no army quarters available and initially we were placed in a holiday B&B in Blackpool. One of my main memories of that time was how cold it was after the heat we'd been living in out in Malaya. Also, once again, it was mainly Mum and us children on our own in Blackpool, whilst Dad went ahead to Catterick Camp, where he was stationed, to sort things out, etc.

I'm not exactly sure just how long we were in Blackpool, but I have a feeling it was possibly a couple of months. From there we moved to a house in Darlington, Durham which was being used by the army as a quarter, until such time as one became vacant in Catterick itself. It was a new build and quite a novelty! It was there that we first had a TV as a family - a surprise from Dad for all of us.

We were living there for about six months I believe, before we moved to Catterick Camp itself. I was there long enough for me to sit the eleven plus, which I somehow managed to pass in spite of all the disruptions in my schooling!

Catterick Camp

The time eventually arrived when there was a quarter available for us at Catterick Camp, and we moved into, what seemed to be, a large old house with five bedrooms - and yet again, another new school! This was another army school in Catterick Camp itself and I was only there for the summer term. Having already got my eleven plus out of the way, I suppose in a way I was just marking time before starting at the senior school in the September of 1955.

I haven't many memories of that school due to the fact that I was there for such a short time. But I do remember feeling a bit lonely and finding it difficult to make friends and get to know the others there. Most of them had been there all through that school year, and possibly longer, and had already had time to make the friendships you do when you're in school. Looking back I think it was quite a pivotal time for me as, unfortunately, I think it reinforced the feeling in me that other people didn't really find me particularly likeable. The senior school I went to was Richmond High School, in Yorkshire - the nearest to Catterick where I lived. I was there just over two years before we moved south once again!

When we moved to Catterick the area we lived in was designated the 'officers' quarters' and we were there because Dad held the rank of captain. From that area we had a strip of woodland which we went down through, over a bridge across the stream that ran through it and then up the other side to another area of quarters. These were where the 'other ranks' lived as they were called - those soldiers not within the 'officer' group. ***Isn't it wonderful to know that in God's sight we are all equal?***

My younger brother and I spent many happy hours playing in those woods! I also discovered that the nearest army 'garrison' church, as it was called, to where we lived wasn't that far away. It was over the bridge and up through the 'other rank' quarters and within walking distance for me. In the 50's there was much more freedom and, although I was only 11yrs old, I joined the choir there and used to walk to and fro on my own.

There seemed a desire within me that made me want to be amongst God's people. From the time I was seven and made, what was possibly a rather childish commitment at Juno's, I tried, whenever possible to be involved. I didn't realise it at the time, but looking back now, I can trace a thread running through the years linking my involvement one way or another. This continued until the time I made a more decisive step into God's Kingdom here on earth, when I was older.

Believe it or not, but we actually had another move during the time we were living in Catterick - although this time I was able to remain at the same school! I'm not absolutely certain, but I think it was because there were less of us, so we didn't need such a big house and moved to a smaller quarter in another part of Catterick. I think my elder brother had gone into the army by then and my eldest sister had also moved away for work - London I believe. My other sister was taking examinations and preparing to move into the nursing fraternity, which also meant that she would be leaving home to go into training.

Moving South Once More to the Wilds of Wiltshire!

We weren't in the second house for very long before we found ourselves on the move again, when Dad was posted to Corsham Ammunition Depot in Wiltshire and it was 'all systems go'! My sister interested in nursing had already gone south to Pirbright in Surrey to train at an orthopaedic hospital - am not sure if it still exists.....

What does remain vivid in my memory, is the drive south from Catterick to Wiltshire. It was on the last day of April and I think it was 1958 but, the reason the day itself stands out, is because we travelled down in a snow blizzard which was somewhat unexpected! Yet again there was no quarter available at Corsham depot.... so we were in an army 'hire' quarter completely away from the depot once more.

The house we moved to was a cottage on a quarter acre of land, rented from a nearby farmer, and in a village called Bulkington in the wilds of Wiltshire. I'm calling it wild because there were only 3 buses a week - apart from the school bus every day in term time! On Thursday there was a bus into Devizes, a nearby market town and the other two buses ran at the beginning and end of the week and they went to Trowbridge, another market town. This was the town that produced Bowyers Wiltshire sausages, up until the time it was closed in 2007, for those who have heard of them. It was also the town where I went to school for the rest of my school days!

BUT God.... is ALWAYS moving in the plan that He's made for us, for you, long before you were even born! The events that happen in your life, both before and after you enter into a living relationship with Him - are all part of His plan and preparation that He has laid out for you in order to fulfil the part He has created for you in His Kingdom.

We had a small village shop there, plus an old medieval, Anglican Church. There was also another old church in the nearest village to us, slightly bigger - both the church and the village, called Keevil. There was an elderly vicar in Keevil who was responsible for both parishes. Neither of the organs in the churches were electronic and both of them had to be pumped to get the air through the pipes in order to play them! When I had the opportunity to have a go, I found it was quite an experience.

I Become Hooked on Farming!

We soon became settled into our country life in Bulkington and I got to know the Farmer and his wife, who owned the house we lived in, and especially their daughter named Ruby. She was in her twenties I believe, and worked on the farm. Gradually I spent more and more of my time on the farm, particularly over the weekends. I eventually got to the point where I would collect the herd of cows from their field on the way up the lane early in the morning, and then help with the milking. I even learned how to milk their Guernsey cow by hand, that was kept mainly for the family to have cream and butter.

Most mornings I went home after milking with cream and eggs for breakfast! Then, depending on what was happening, I would return later to help with the various jobs on the farm. I do remember in particular that I first learned to drive a tractor there on the farm, at the age of 13. Not surprisingly this all resulted in me becoming more and more interested in moving into some form of agriculture when I left school.

When I was slightly older, around 15 I believe, I had the opportunity to attend a sort of 'taster' session at Lacock Agricultural College in that part of Wiltshire. I was quite smitten with farming by then and later applied, and was accepted, for a full blown course at an agricultural college elsewhere in the country.

To attend, I had to complete a year of practical work on a farm - one which kept records of milk yields and crops etc. This, unfortunately cut out spending my year on the farm up the lane as, back at the end of the fifties not all farms kept full records, and this was one of the ones that didn't!

Moving Again - Corsham

But, I'm getting ahead of myself! Before going to complete a practical year on a farm, I had to complete my education. At the same time a quarter became vacant and we moved to the army depot at Corsham. I was somewhat devastated as you can probably imagine, as it took me away from the access to the farm where I spent as much of my spare time as I was able to.

At least I didn't have to change school this time, and was able to catch a train from Corsham to Trowbridge every day. In some ways, I suppose it helped me concentrate on my studies for my 'O Level' examinations coming up, without the distraction of wanting to be up on the farm all the time!

What springs to mind is: "For My thoughts are not your thoughts, neither are your ways My ways, says the Lord." through the prophet Isaiah.

I completed my 'O Levels' at the school in Trowbridge but, before leaving there was one event that took place that had some bearing on something that happened a bit later on. I was messing around at home, jumped up in the air and when I landed I managed to somehow bend the big toe backwards on my right foot. I have no idea how! It hurt a great deal initially but it gradually got better and I forgot about it....

My Aborted Attempt at Farming

With help from the school, or possibly the Agricultural college where I obtained a place (I honestly can't remember which, and maybe it was neither!) - I managed to get a placement for my practical year. The farm, I believe, was roughly 100 acres in size, and was situated near the town of Cricklade. It wasn't very far from Swindon and still in Wiltshire. The farmers were a young couple with a young child - a little girl.

From memory, my primary job was milking the cows every morning, which entailed an early start, and evening. I also had to keep records of the milk yields of the various cows. Through the day, in between the milking sessions, I took part over a period of time in most of the usual activities on a farm. These included keeping the milking parlour clean and hygienic, collecting eggs, etc and mucking out the chicken houses. And in the summer months there was the harvesting of the hay and straw and getting it put away for the winter.

One thing that happened - and this makes me sound somewhat accident prone - but I got kicked by one of the cows! It caught me on the inside of my thigh, just above my right knee - and left me with a hoof size shaped bruise, which was painful and not in a hurry to go!

About half way through the year the farmer and his wife found out that they were expecting a second child. They decided at this stage to ask me to split my time. This would work out with me continuing to work on the farm, but only part-time - the rest of the time I would work in the house, plus helping with the children..... They would then employ a young man to help with the work on the farm.

Unfortunately for me, this would mean that I wouldn't be able to fulfil the statutory year of practical work that I needed to complete, in order to take up the place at the agricultural college. As it was already half way through the year, it wasn't possible to move to another farm and complete a year's practical work - before I was due to take up the place at college. I had no option, but to leave the farm and return home.

So - What next?

From the farm I returned home to live with my parents once more at Corsham - I would have been 17 years old at that time. I needed to get a job and, although I'd always maintained I didn't want to work in an office, I ended up working as a temporary Clerical Assistant in the Civil Service. The place I worked at was Copenacre, a Royal Navy Supply Depot near Corsham.

However, I realise now that the Lord had new skills for me to learn and the time had come to move into a new season in my life.

Actually I ended up working in office based jobs for the next 4 years - but fortunately I didn't know at the time that that would be the case! For close on 3 of those years I was in the Civil Service. First of all as a Temporary Clerical Assistant, which was at Copenacre; and then as a Temporary Clerical Officer for nearly two years at Bramley, not far from Basingstoke in Hampshire - where there was yet another ammunition depot...

The change in area, as you might have guessed, was because Dad had once again been moved. During his time at Corsham the Army Fire Service was civilianised and became, I believe, a branch of the Civil Service. The main change for us as a family was that we no longer had to live in an army quarter on camp - but were able to buy a property and live somewhere of our own choice. So, when I returned to live at home, we were living in Chippenham a town not far from Corsham.

But I'm getting ahead of myself once again.... as I said earlier, I wasn't too keen on working in an office so, when I finished my farming 'career' - I looked around for something else to do! I suppose with my background as part of an army family, it's not too much of a surprise that I looked in the direction of the army!! With Dad's help, I made some investigations concerning applying for entry as a female army officer and was successful in being accepted for going for a three day assessment course. And, it's probably not too much of a surprise to hear that, at the age of 17 1/2 years of age - I wasn't accepted; although I was told I could try again when I was older! After that I thought I would try for the police force, but again I was too young even to apply, and I have a suspicion that I was possibly a bit short as well. Hence me ending up at Copenacre!

Bramley and New Skills

When Dad was posted to Bramley we bought a house in Basingstoke. There was a vacancy at the depot for a Temporary

Clerical Officer, which I was able to apply for with the 'O' levels I had, and I got transferred over. I was able to travel in to work with Dad each day which was very helpful. Initially I was in the 'stocktaking and reconciliation' section. The men working in the depot would count the ammunition etc in store and send the numbers to the office - and we had to balance (reconcile) them with what was in the record books.

Not exactly an exhilarating job at the age of 18 - so, when a vacancy came up in the wages department, I jumped at it, and was fortunate to find I had more of a head for figures than I realised, and also enjoyed it. I was involved in the preparation of the payrolls using PAYE and, from the Bramley office, we did the payrolls for several surrounding army bases as well.

During my time working at Bramley we moved again - this time to a bungalow in Old Basing, which was nearer to the depot than our house in Basingstoke. Whilst we were in Basingstoke I joined the choir at St Michael's Church and was able to continue going there when we moved. Having been involved in the Brownies during my time in Malaya, I joined the local Guide company in Old Basing. To my amazement I ended up leading it in due course, owing to the fact that the Guide Captain was leaving, and there was no one else willing to replace her. This was another first, as I hadn't really worked with young people before - and I enjoyed it.

From a natural viewpoint I would say that the fact that I began to get 'itchy feet' again as we arrived in the year 1964 and I reached the great age of 20, was due to my army background and moving on every couple of years!

This actually proved to be the Lord's intervention and the way He took me out of the plan I had worked out, to spend my life in the agricultural arena - although I didn't realise it at the time! I believe that, although only a child of seven at the time I made that commitment to follow Jesus whilst in the Juno's, GOD took it seriously. My plan to go into farming wasn't something I had talked to God about - it was something I thought I'd like to do. What I didn't realise was, that He had other plans for me.... and farming wasn't part of them!

I have come to learn over the years that nothing, absolutely nothing, is ever wasted in God's economy. Over these years when I first left school, which might seem a time when I was chopping and changing in respect of work, I realise now that I was learning skills that I would need in the future to enable me to fulfil Father's plans for me! And this continued during the next few years.....

Remember, when you suddenly find that nothing you'd got planned actually happens, that it could easily be that Father has something else that's completely different on His heart for you! But don't look back and conclude that what you've been doing is a waste of time. You can be pretty certain that you've been learning skills that you'll need at some stage in your life as you walk forward with the Lord.

Chapter 2/2 God Changes My Life

Moving On

I believe I looked into the possibility of working overseas (through VSO) but it wasn't time yet for the Lord to move me in that direction - and I actually only got as far as London! I was accepted by BP to work as a Wages Clerk in their Accounts Department at BP House in Moorgate and started working there in June 1964. I moved into the YWCA in Great Russell Street, and not too far from Oxford Street. At first I was in a sort of dormitory with several other girls, and then Jenny, someone I became good friends with, and I decided to share a room.

Not long after moving into the YWCA I was surprised to discover that there was a chapel in the hostel, although I shouldn't have been as, after all, it is a Christian Association for Young Women. I also found out that they held a 15 minute 'slot' every evening for those who wanted to get together. I felt drawn to go and, once more from a natural point of view it might have been that I wanted to meet people - but I'm sure that it was God that drew me, due to the result it brought about in my life!

I did get to know people and, in particular a music student called Catherine who was studying at the Guildhall School of Music. She took quite a lead in the evening sessions and if there was any singing she, understandably in view of the fact she was studying music, would accompany us. I got to know her quite well and she actually ended up being used by God in the beginning of my walk with the Lord.

There was a scheme started in London in 1964 around that time, that set out to link young people in their late teens and early twenties, and especially students, with some of the elderly, and often lonely people that lived there. Catherine asked me if I'd like to join her in visiting an older person and, when I agreed, put us down to be linked up with someone. And so began a time in my life when I definitely 'moved on' - in a far more radical way than just moving on my own to London!

Born Again into the Kingdom

Catherine and I started to visit an elderly widow together on a Sunday, although to my shame I can't remember her name or exactly where it was that she lived. We always walked there from Great Russel Street so I guess it was fairly central. The lady's husband had fought in the First World War and been injured - she described it that 'he had been shot through the foot and gassed', although we were never quite sure if it was one incident or two..... We worked out that it must have been mustard gas and believe that after the war his health was never very good as a result because of it having affected his lungs.

Catherine used to go to church at the Methodist Central Hall, very near to Westminster Abbey, and invited me to go with her to the evening meeting after our Sunday afternoon visits. As you can imagine, we got to know each other pretty well from spending a good percentage of our Sundays together - plus meeting up at the evening chapel meetings, not to mention often having meals together. The YWCA was a Hostel, so we also had our meals provided - at least breakfast and an evening meal, am not too sure about lunches!

My friend Catherine never hid the fact that she was a born again believer and would often talk to me about her faith. I wasn't one for talking at length, and I was quite happy to let her do most of the talking! What struck me most, and always stayed with me, is the way she had of talking about Jesus as though she knew Him and that they regularly had conversations together. It was the first time I had ever met anyone who spoke in this way and it had quite an affect on me, which is why I remember it so much.

Quite early on in 1965, at the Sunday evening meeting at Central Hall, there was a different sort of message shared in the sermon - one that I didn't remember hearing before, although I must have heard something similar back in Tonbridge when I was seven, before we went off to Malaya. I know now, although I didn't then, that it was in fact a Gospel message. I couldn't tell you the specific content of the message, but it resulted in everyone being asked to stand and an invitation being given to those who wanted to, to give their heart to Jesus and commit their lives to Him. Then those who had done so were invited to come forward to the front of the church. I took the step in my heart - but I was up in the balcony and there was no way I was going down!

The seed, that was planted in me way back as a seven year old in Tonbridge in the Juno's, had been watered and was bearing fruit. I believe the decision I made in the Methodist Central Hall that Sunday night was when I was truly born again of the Spirit and entered the Kingdom of God. What I didn't do that night, and have always regretted the fact, I didn't confess the step of

faith that I had taken. As a result, I want to encourage you always to share and speak up and say what God is doing in your life - whether it's when you were first born again, or as you grow in your walk of faith. By speaking it out it somehow firms up what you say and makes it more concrete and real in your life - otherwise it can easily be hidden within you and, in time you can wonder whether it actually even happened!

In fact this was highlighted to me only a week or so later! Some of the other Christians I had met at the YWCA attended All Soul's Church, Langham Place where John Stott was vicar, a well known minister. They invited me to go with them to the evening meeting. I realised why when he started preaching, as he also gave a gospel message and there was an altar call at the end! When we came out afterwards my friends looked at me in a very enquiring way, and asked what I thought about what he'd said? That was when I realised that they'd known it was going to be an evangelistic message - and had taken me along hoping I'd respond..... I was rather 'put on the spot' and of course I then had to share with them that I'd already taken the step. I also shared with Catherine, as I hadn't told her either!

My First Experience of Sharing Jesus

I do so often feel that the Lord has such a sense of humour, because I agreed to help at a children's outreach summer camp (although not under canvas) in the summer of 1965. The incredible thing was that Catherine had invited me to go, and I'd accepted, before that Sunday evening when I finally committed my life to Jesus!

It was run by the BMMF (Bible and Medical Missionary Fellowship, known as Interserve since 1987) and a friend of Catherine's from Cornwall, Marion Yelland was attending to help in her capacity as a missionary working in India. At the camp each dormitory with eight or nine girls in, was given two 'helpers' to lead them and it was Marion that I was actually teamed up with! We would lead them in a Quiet Time each morning - reading the Bible and praying, which in fact was pretty much as new to me as it was to most of the girls! I learned a great deal on that first children's camp I helped at. I say 'first' because I continued to go for a few years after that.

All Change

That year of 1965 was one that probably had the most changes in one year of my life up until that point!. Of course the biggest and most important decision was the one that took me into God's Kingdom and I became a citizen of heaven - even though I continued to be a citizen of this world at the same time. It wasn't long after that before there were more changes in my life. My original misgivings at working in an office rose to the surface again and I began to wonder what I should do and, most important of all, I began praying and asking God what He wanted me to do!

A copy of the 'Lady' magazine came into my possession - am not certain if a kind colleague at the office got it for me, or just made the suggestion that I might get some ideas from it. Anyway, I came across this job advertisement for a post working in a children's home run by the Church of England. It was situated in Hampstead Garden Suburb in north London - a place I had heard of but had never been to..... To cut a long story short the application and acceptance went through pretty quickly and it was arranged that I would start at the beginning of October in the position of Senior Assistant Housemother - in spite of the fact that I was only 21, without any experience!

I finished my year at BP in the June of 1965 and spent a couple of months 'temping' as a wages clerk for the Alfred Marks Staff Bureau in London. I finished there in good time to attend the BMMF camp in August based at Overstone School - a private boarding school near Northampton. I wasn't aware of it then, but the Lord was going to take me back to that school as a teacher in the future. Amazing! But I'm getting ahead of myself....

Hampstead and the Children's Home

The day I arrived at the Children's Home to start work there - I was told that part of my duties was to feed everyone, 20 to 25 people a day. I'm not kidding when I say that I nearly turned round and went home!

Believe me, when I say that I'm sure it was God's grace, and God's grace alone that kept me there!! If you're really serious about wanting to move forward in your walk (relationship) with Jesus, you need to start learning as soon as possible that you have to start talking (praying) to the Lord about everything you do, and learn how to let the Holy Spirit guide and teach you. Unfortunately it doesn't happen over night - but then learning new things, usually takes time if you're going to learn them properly.....

I started my 'learning' in earnest, that first day at the Home - and am still learning well over 50 years later! I'm not confessing to being a slow learner, I hasten to add, but learning to be taught and guided by the Spirit is something, like many others, that will continue until I go to Glory. This is because your Father is always wanting to take you into a deeper relationship with Him as you learn more and more about how to do things His way.

Actually the Housemother gave me a lot of help with the cooking initially, which I was very grateful to the Lord for - particularly working out the menus and ordering the food required. I was also grateful that I came from a large family as, when we were all at home, there were 7 of us in total - this helped me greatly as my mother had taught me how to cook for the family. And, most of all, I thanked the Lord that I enjoyed cooking and, once I got over the initial shock, I actually enjoyed cooking for everybody - although it took me a while to get used to cooking on an Aga!

Fifty odd years later I am amazed that the post I held as the senior assistant meant that, when the Houseparents weren't on duty - I was the one responsible. In some ways I suppose it was as well that at the time I didn't fully realise the amount of responsibility I was carrying! The children in care at the home were all boys, ranging from the age of 3 up to 15 - some with very sad backgrounds. And even the junior assistant, 18 years old I think, actually came from a broken home herself as well.

It was hard work - long days and only one day off in the week, which wasn't on a weekend. This was because of having the majority of boys at home from school at that point; although I did have an hour or two off at some stage of each day, when things were running smoothly that is! As well as one day a week, I had a 'long weekend' off, once a quarter. It certainly wasn't a job for the faint hearted.... I don't believe I'd consciously thought about it, but I believe I realised that my time there wasn't going to be long term. I somehow knew in my spirit, that it was the start of something completely different in my life, though I had no idea exactly what!

I went home to stay with my parents for my first long weekend off - which consisted of going on Friday and returning the following Tuesday. By this time my parents were living in Seabrook, just along the coast from Folkestone in Kent, and dad was Fire Officer in that area based at the Junior Leaders unit. Whilst I was home my mother found an advertisement in the local paper, in which they were asking for 'mature' students to train to be teachers. My mother had always wanted to teach but her mother, my grandmother, was a war widow from the First World War and money was scarce - and she had ended up as a hairdresser.

Mum showed me the advert and I realised that she would be thrilled if I did something about it! She didn't push it at me and I know us five children were fortunate in having parents who would give us advice in looking for job options, but never put pressure on us to move in a particular career direction, unless that was what we wanted. I have to be honest when I say that I never had any desire to teach, or any intention to do so either!

However, it seemed that the Lord had other ideas.... During the course of the weekend this advertisement, and what it contained, kept returning to my mind on a regular basis - to the point where I began to get irritated by it! The details of an office in Folkestone, where more information could be obtained, was included in the advert - and by the time Monday came my dad agreed to take me there to find out more. Basically, I realised that I had completely lost my peace over the whole situation - and realised it wouldn't return until I found out more about it all.

I was too young a believer at that point to fully realise what the Lord was doing which, in fact, was simply guiding and gently pushing me in the direction He wanted me to go. It's wonderful how our Father leads and guides us and shows us what He wants us to do. All of us need to be sensitive to the nudges of the Holy Spirit. Be aware, as you are walking in the new life that Jesus has given you - be aware and alert to His guidance, and don't brush off the thoughts and promptings that come to you from the Holy Spirit, unless or until you're absolutely sure that they aren't what He is saying to you! Learn to listen and be sensitive to all Father wants to say to you in every area of your life.

Well, I was given a whole load of information, plus paperwork on my visit to the office - including application forms and details of various colleges, etc. I was still feeling uncomfortable about it all but now it was discomfort from thinking that maybe it was something I should do, although not overjoyed at the thought of it!

I believe my visit home was in the December of 1965, not long before Christmas which, as you can imagine was a very busy time at the Home! It didn't give me a great deal of time to think about the future and applying for teacher training - if that was the direction the Lord was taking me in! I knew from the paperwork I'd been given that, once we were into the new year, I needed to get an application in if I intended to act on what, by then I was beginning to realise, was probably where the Lord was leading me.

It's important for us to recognise when the Holy Spirit is leading us - and equally important to recognise when He is not! As you walk forward with the Lord you will learn, and we are all unique in the sight of God and we learn in different ways, to recognise when it's the Lord, when it's yourself, or when it's the enemy. Sometimes you have to move forward and find you've made a mistake - but, amazingly, it's all part of the learning process.

So.... early January 1966 saw me begin to take tentative steps towards filling in the paperwork and making a decision on which college to apply for. I have to say that I still wasn't completely comfortable about it and the thought of standing up in a classroom to teach was a scary prospect. But, at the same time, I found my thinking was changing and, because my desire was to be obedient to the Lord (I realise now how, when we start to love Jesus - He changes the way we look at things!), I was no longer fighting against it and part of me was even starting to be excited!

The following weeks saw me becoming more confident and efficient in the work and relationships with the boys in the Home. And at the same time, on a completely different level, I completed the filling in of the application for a place at a teacher training college. Needless to say, my mother was thrilled, and both she and dad gave me as much help as they could from a distance.... I had to put three possibilities of colleges I'd like to attend - in order of preference. Canterbury was my first choice, with Salisbury my third - unfortunately I cannot remember the one in the middle!

The applications were duly processed and cleared through the system and, in due course, I heard that I was being offered a place to train at the College of Sarum St Michael in Salisbury, Wiltshire. This wasn't my first choice, in fact my last, but.... by this time my whole attitude had been turned around by the Lord, and I was just so pleased to be given a place. And then I had it confirmed that I'd successfully been offered a grant to cover my three years of training. God is so good!

I remained at the Home until August of that year, and then embarked on my teacher training course in the September. I enjoyed my time working at the children's home and knew I would miss the boys there. A lot happened in those months but, one thing in particular I need to share, because of the impact it had on my later life.

One thing I did find I had more time for while at the Home was reading as, obviously, I wasn't on duty for the whole of every day. I began reading some of the Christian classics, such as the life of Hudson Taylor and other men and women who went overseas in the early years of mission that was embarked on from this country. At this stage I can't remember how I came across these various books - but I got hooked! But it was the life of Amy Carmichael in particular that the Lord spoke to me through, and her books about rescuing children from the Indian temples in Southern India.

From a natural viewpoint I think that the fact that, on the way back from Malaya, we spent a night in Calcutta, played a large part in my interest in India. We were taken back to the airport, from the hotel where we had stayed overnight, very early in the morning. I have never forgotten the sight of families, yes I said families (although I believe there were adults and young people fending for themselves alone as well) getting up and starting a new day - from the places on the streets where they had slept overnight. I think this played a part in my interest in India and especially how Amy Carmichael was helping so many needy children, and encouraging others to join her.

With all the input I received on India it's no real surprise for you to know that the Lord spoke to me about going there in due course, and planted a seed of missionary zeal in my heart. But, and it's a big BUT, GOD is never in a hurry and it turned out to be 18 years before I went to India - and, once again, I'm jumping ahead too far to another part of my story way into the future!

Another instance of how the Lord weaves what appear quite isolated incidences into our lives - and then uses them at a later date to speak to us. Be alert to what is going on around you and 'see' and 'hear' what is happening. You never know when the Lord might bring it back to your remembrance in order to use you in a particular way that He has planned!

Chapter 2/3 Entering the World of Education

Student Life in Salisbury

Embarking on studies to be a teacher, I was classed as a 'mature' student in spite of only being 22 years of age at the time, because I'd been working in the 'real' world beforehand! I was excited about going to college - by the time I got there!! There was an element within the excitement of slight trepidation, as to whether I would be accepted as I was older than most of the students - even the third year students.....

I was also looking forward to meeting up with other Christians there and spending time with them. I did find though, that I'd made one mistake out of lack of knowledge and the fact that the believers I'd known up until that point had all been keen to go on with the Lord. I had assumed that all believers were 'keen'..... but it was rather a rude awakening when I began to realise that some of the believers I was meeting in college, had other priorities in their lives that appeared to come first and, to a certain extent, seemed more important to them.

We need to remind ourselves as often as possible that our relationship and walk with the Lord is NOT a part-time connection - it's FULL-TIME. Is your relationship with Jesus there for your convenience - ie mainly when you're in need of His help? OR, is your relationship with Him functioning on a 24 hour basis - one where He is part of all that is taking place in

your life? Let me say that this doesn't always happen overnight, although it can; but sometimes it's a growing realisation that the only relationship you really want with Jesus is for Him to be part of your life in everything that takes place. It's a relationship that will continue to grow and become deeper as you walk with Him and learn to love Him more and more - not for what He does for you, but because of Who He is.

Well, after working and being independent, it was a bit of a shock to my system to find that as a student I was, for the most part, being told what I should be doing! I lived in college for my first and third year, but was boarded out for the middle year. I did my teacher training at the College of Sarum St Michael, which was situated in the Cathedral Close - opposite the main doors into Salisbury Cathedral. Unfortunately it closed in 1978 and is now, I believe, used as a museum. However, that was no where on the horizon during my time there.

Where do I start to give you some idea of my three years as a student that, once again, turned my life right around?? Amazingly, I think now that I can probably sum it up in one word 'learning' - although I'm not so sure that's what I would have said at the time! Now, you could say that's too obvious because I was learning - that was what I was there for, to learn to be a teacher. But, I think that's the word I've used because, thinking about it now I'm realising, in a way I never have before (possibly because I've never needed to think about it in any depth) that what I learned in those three years was far, far more than simply learning to be a teacher - if learning to be a teacher can ever be simple!

Learning to Live Differently

So, what did I learn in those three years that was over and above my studies to become a teacher? Apart, that is, from realising that actually it was something I wanted to do! There was a Christian Union at the college and several of us who got to know each other started attending a Free Evangelical Church in Salisbury and became part of the Body of Christ there. For me this was particularly exciting because previously I'd not been part of a body of believers on a regular basis over a period of time, and I began to learn a great deal and became much stronger in my walk with the Lord. Some of us actually went up from the church to help with the counselling when Billy Graham held his London crusade in June,1967 - quite an experience!

I got to know a second year student who also knew the Lord and we became good friends. I can remember us talking late at night about our faith and a whole load of other things beside.... It was usually in her room, so she was in bed and I'd sit on the floor and we more often than not were in the dark. Probably sounds a bit bizarre but for me, that was the first time that I ever remember starting to talk freely to someone - I actually began to open up and talk about how I felt about things. And because it was dark I couldn't be seen as I talked, and somehow it enabled me to voice things I would never have done otherwise.

Gradually, over those years in college, and the many years following, the Lord helped me to learn to open myself up more, both to Him and to the people He brought me in contact with. There are times even now, after all these years, when I don't

always find it is easy to speak up - especially about my personal feelings about things. But God.... there really is nothing that is too hard for the Lord to do in your life if you ask for His help, and He's always ready and willing to help - if you're willing to ask Him. Don't be proud - I encourage you to have a willing heart, and ask. Yes, it may be uncomfortable at times - but far better to ask, and go on; rather than keep quiet and and get stuck.

In order to share another area of learning, I need to go back a little to fill in some details that I didn't include earlier, concerning some health challenges that I experienced. I believe I did recount how I bent over the big toe on my right foot, just before I finished school - however I didn't include what followed on not that long afterwards when we had moved to Chippenham. I ended up with my right leg wrapped in sticky plaster from below the knee, right down to my toes - for about three weeks I think, to try and get rid of the pain radiating from the toe in question! I tell you it's no joke when it comes to removing the plaster - the hairs on my leg had grown and got attached, and when they ripped off the plaster in one go, it was extremely painful. Mind you it did seem pretty well ok for a while after that.... Remember, this was during the time before I came to know the Lord and my attitude to my health was very different - at that stage I hadn't met up with the 'Healer'!!

We moved to Basingstoke and I started getting pain in my back at the base of my spine. They took some x-rays at the hospital but couldn't really find anything wrong, and it wasn't till later I found out that they'd told my parents it was psychological - although they did strap me in a sort of jacket / corset for a while, but that wasn't much help either. Eventually I was more or less left to get on with it....

The reason I've explained this at this point is because, after I started at college and was involved in a certain amount of physical education - both the leg and the back took a turn for the worse and I ended up back at the hospital for investigation. This time, however, I had friends praying it would get sorted. After x-raying the toe that had been badly bent, they found that the small bone at the base of the toe had split and was causing the pain because of the angle it was at. They put this right with a local anaesthetic and some wriggling around of the bone - it never has been any more trouble! Praise the Lord!

The back wasn't quite so simple. They x-rayed it again but from different angles and found that I actually had six bones in the part of the bottom of the spine known as the coccyx, instead of five, and they thought that was what was causing the pain and discomfort. They manipulated my spine under an anaesthetic, and then decided to put me in a plaster cast for six weeks. Fortunately for part of this time I was home between terms, but the whole experience was rather challenging as the plaster was from just below the bust to the top of the legs - rather restrictive to say the least! My college friends were so good in the help they gave me..... I couldn't sit up or lay down in bed on my own, and they took turns morning and evening in helping me.

Afterwards I had physio etc but unfortunately none of the treatment was very successful and the medics said there wasn't anything else they could do! As you've probably realised by now - the fact that this all happened in my first year at college, was quite a challenge on top of my studies, and everything else going on in my life..... and it was difficult to cope with it all.

BUT GOD.... enabled me to cope and I began to learn that with God all things are possible - even living with pain. And I began to have my first real experience of learning that my Father never allows me to be in a situation without giving me the strength to cope with it. If you are facing difficulties in your life at the time you are reading this - turn to your Heavenly Father for help. It might not come in the way you might prefer it to, but He will help you and take you through it (yes, very often it's a 'taking through' rather than a 'taking out of'). In my case I longed to be free of the pain and leave it all behind - but at that point the Lord helped me and took me through it. The next part of my story concerning my back, comes at a later date....

I think I need to add here that I'm not saying I was 'on top' and 'coping' with all that was happening all the time! Believe me, when I say I had my bad days and wondered where it would all end up.... But I was learning to turn to my Father for the help I needed and He was always there to help me. It was a 'learning curve' for me and one I go on learning in different ways with different challenges. And it will be a learning curve for you when you're in need of help, so don't give up if you're finding the learning difficult. I came out stronger - and you will too.

Teaching Practice

Each of the three years I was training, I was sent out on 'Teaching Practice' which was exactly what it says it is. I was training for teaching the top junior and senior age group - and ended up with practices for both age groups. I did two weeks with a top class in a junior school (it would be called Yr 6 in today's National Curriculum - but this was a long time before that started!) in my first year in college. Both the other practices were in senior schools, my main interest - four weeks in the middle year; and six weeks in my final year.

None of my practices were easy, and weren't meant to be! It really was a case of 'learning on the job'..... and very nerve racking at times. One memory especially stays with me, from my final practice in a large comprehensive school, of a particularly lively class who decided they wanted to behave for me when my tutor came to sit in on my lesson. The trouble was that they felt the only way to behave was to keep absolutely quiet - and I ended up being told by my tutor that I needed more 'interaction' with the class, who were14/15 yr olds! As I said it wasn't easy, but over time I began to have moments when I would realise that, in fact, I was beginning to enjoy what I was doing.

I have to confess that, at the time, I never fully realised just what the Lord did in me concerning teaching! As I said earlier I never, ever had any desire whatsoever to become a teacher. If anything, I think I was always horrified at the thought of it. The amazing thing is that, as I was obedient in following the Lord's leading in this, so He gradually changed my whole attitude and thinking towards teaching. And, as I worked my way through my teaching practices, I began to find, as I said before, that I began to enjoy myself!

Believe me, when I say that it could only be through the Holy Spirit working in me to change me, and because the Lord knew

all along that it was His choice for me. He gave me the strength and the knowledge and, in due course, the pleasure of being a teacher. If you're being challenged about doing something you're not particularly keen on doing - please don't automatically dismiss it. Talk to the Lord about it and, most of all, ask the necessary questions regarding whether it might be something He wants you to do - even if you think you'd never be able to. I'm continually learning that when I say 'I can't' - He shows me that 'He can', as long as I do the bit that He shows me to do.

Growing in the Lord

I can't end the account of my time at Salisbury without sharing with you how the Lord met with me in a completely new way, and with another learning curve.

As my three years as a student went by, I found myself in contact with many more believers and learned a great deal more about the Body of Christ. I attended a few conferences with friends from Salisbury - run especially for Christian college students. And I also went and helped at more children camps run by BMMF - only by then I knew a little more about what I was doing. And in one of the summer breaks I went and worked at the London office of BMMF for a while - where my office experience was put to good use.

I got to know a girl at college whose Christian experience was rooted in an Assemblies of God church. I don't think I had realised, until I went to college and also through studying Divinity as my main subject, just how much variety and number of denominations there were in the church. My background had mainly been Anglican, Church of England - so I had a lot to learn. Anyway, back to my friend, through whom I heard all about the baptism of the Holy Spirit - and I think it was quite possibly for the first time. I might have heard of it previously, but this was definitely the time that I registered it and began to want to know more. I can't be absolutely certain, but I think it was in my last year at college, when I was back in college accommodation.

I remember three stages taking place in connection with this. I remember my friend (and if you ever end up reading this and make the connection - I apologise for not being able to remember your name!) explaining to me all about the baptism of the Spirit - and asking me if I'd like her to pray for me. The second stage was her actually praying for me - and nothing happening! The third stage, and I'm not sure if this was the same day or a day or so later.... was me kneeling by my bed, before actually going to bed, and asking the Lord to show me how to speak in tongues. Then I got into bed and lay thinking about it all, and then vaguely remembering something having been said about singing in tongues. I always loved to sing and wondered if it would be easier - so I lay in bed, not really the best position, opened my mouth to see if I could sing in tongues.... and found that's exactly what happened! Praise the Lord! And then I found I could also speak in tongues as well.

What a gift given to us freely by our Heavenly Father, although I confess that at that stage I had no idea what a wonderful gift I'd been given - or that it was so much more than being able to speak in tongues, wonderful as that is. Once again a learning curve and one I continue to learn about, even after all

these years. If you feel you want to know more about this wonderful gift of the baptism in the Spirit, either because you've not experienced it or because you feel there's more than you've so far experienced - then I would encourage you to talk to the Lord about it first of all, always our first 'port of call'! But, if you feel the need to speak to someone, find a friend or minister you know and trust, and ask their advice - making sure first that they have experience themselves in the baptism in the Spirit, or it could become confusing....

From Training to School

Of course you can only train for so long and my course was to obtain a Teaching Certificate, which was covered in the three years at Salisbury. The time came when I needed to start looking for a teaching position in an actual school! The majority of students in my college year were leaving at the end of their three year training, and looking for teaching positions pretty well all over the UK. There were a few who wanted to stay on another year and study for their B Ed (Bachelor of Education) degree, but I wasn't one of them!

I eventually got an interview, and was accepted in due course as an Assistant Teacher, at Mount Pleasant Girl's School, Upper Clapton in the East End, London. In fact they were short staffed and asked if I could start straight away for the remainder of the summer term. I was pleased to start early as I felt it was God's provision for me at the time before starting at the beginning of the Autumn term in September. So I worked at the school from July of the summer term. And after that was based at my parent's through the summer holidays - apart from helping again at the BMMF Children's Camp that summer. I didn't know then that it would be for the last time.

Of course I also had to find somewhere to live, within reasonable and easy access on public transport to the school. I ended up with a semi bed-sit in the top half of a house in Homerton, Hackney, East London. I say semi as I had a sort of studio room for living and sleeping and with washing facilities - and a separate kitchen which, at the point I moved in, hadn't actually got a sink. This meant I had to use the sink etc in my studio room. I had the use of the bathroom downstairs for taking a bath.

The couple who rented it to me were very pleasant. He worked somewhere that involved shift work and was often working at night. His wife was stone deaf and I think one of the reasons they wanted to rent out the upstairs, was in order to help her feel safer at night when her husband was away working, and she was on her own.

The month of July at the school was helpful in giving me an overview of the school as a whole, although I realised it possibly wasn't going to be easy! However, I did thank the Lord for giving me the opportunity and for preparing me for what He was taking me into. At the same time I discovered that there was a very lively Anglican Church across from where I was living, at the other side of another school, not the one I was going to be teaching at. This was definitely a gift from the Lord and it wasn't very long before I felt welcomed and made to feel part of the church family there.

Let's face it - the Lord had done it again! He had made provision in every way for the next season of my life..... made me aware of what I was facing in the school He was taking me to; given me somewhere to live physically and, most important of all, somewhere to 'live' spiritually. I don't think I realised it then, but certainly have come to realise it through the years, that the most important place is where the Lord wants us to have our spiritual home, during each season of our lives.

I would encourage you to always ask the Lord for help and search for that as a priority! We, you and I, need to be planted in a community of the Lord's people that enables us to grow. I'm not saying that there won't be times, as you grow in maturity in your faith and relationship with Jesus, that He won't take you to places where you're the one who helps with the growth in others. But when, and if, that happens do make sure it's the Lord who's taking you, and not your own desires and plans. If it's Him who takes you there - you'll also find yourself growing as you reach out and teach those around you.

CHAPTER 3

Dealing With Stagnation

3/1 Life at a Standstill Until God Steps In

Full Time Teaching in a School

My time to start full time teaching at Mount Pleasant School had arrived, but it helped so much that I'd already spent some time there! As I said earlier, I realised during my time at the school at the end of the summer term that it wasn't going to be easy. It was a very mixed community, with quite a wide variety of girls from different ethnicities. The post of assistant teacher that I was given consisted of teaching Religious Education throughout the school, teaching some general subjects and, in particular, being responsible for a second year (today it would be called year 8) remedial class.

It was only when I looked back at a later date, after I had become an experienced teacher, that I fully realised how wrong it was to give a probationary teacher (which is what I was) a large remedial class containing 29 students. Nowadays, special needs classes would never have that number of youngsters in one class - or have been given to a probationer, an inexperienced teacher. Unfortunately, at the time I started teaching in 1969, it was not unusual - and there were no classroom assistants either! The other unfortunate thing was that the Head Teacher seemed to lack any understanding of the situation she'd placed me in - and I wasn't given a great deal of help.

I would love to be able to now relate to you a wonderful testimony of how I drew on God's strength to cope, and share with you how He enabled me to walk in victory through it all.... In reality I have to confess that I didn't do very well and admit that I ended up failing miserably. But again, I'm jumping ahead of myself and giving you the final outcome. It was all new to me and, although only a young Christian, I did my utmost to bring honour to the Lord during my time at the school. And I met some lovely girls there, as well as some very difficult ones, although even as inexperienced as I was, I realised that some of the behaviour displayed was as a result of their own difficulties that they were facing.

One girl sticks in my mind in particular. She was in the Remedial class that I spent the majority of my time with, so she would have probably been aged 12. She was from the Caribbean, sent to England on her own to live with her father and older siblings - not knowing any of them very well and she had left her mother and younger siblings behind in Jamaica. Her grasp of spoken English was poor and her written English was even worse. During the time I worked with her, I found it became an achievement to get her to actually put on a page a copied line of writing. She found the situation even more frustrating than I did and it would often end in her exploding in anger over the situation she found herself in.

There was another girl that I also particularly remember - again from a Caribbean background. She was constantly falling asleep over her desk and achieved very little work. When we eventually got to the root of the problem we found that, during the time she was at home, she was basically treated as a skivvy. She was the odd one out in the part of the family living in England and, as such, was at the bottom of the 'pecking order' and ended up doing a great deal of the work in the home. It was simply because she was so exhausted that she kept falling asleep as soon she sat on a chair without having to get on with any housework, etc. I believe the school had to get the authorities involved re her care.

My New Church Family

I soon became involved in the lively Anglican Church near to where I was living and was made very welcome by the community there. It was led by John and Angela who had four children. As you can possibly imagine, leading a church in Homerton in East London is no easy task! Even back then, at the end of the 60's and into the 70's, the drug culture was growing at a rapid rate of knots. A difficult situation when you had children and never knew what they might be offered! I remember Angela saying how many of their fellow clergy sent their children to schools out of the area or even to boarding school. But they had believed the Lord had said they needed to send their children to the local schools. They didn't feel they should separate themselves and be different to the people they lived and worked amongst.

I found that John and Angela were completely 'sold out' to Jesus and just being around them and part of the church they led, made me hungry and want to know Jesus more deeply. There were quite a few different groups that met through the week and the one I especially found helpful was the Monday evening Bible Study and sharing group that Angela led. They also always had an 'open door' to their home so there were always other people there besides their own family.

A Break from School

I acknowledged earlier that I didn't walk in victory during this time at Mount Pleasant School, but I didn't actually go 'straight under' either! My regular contact with the Lord's people, and the support that they gave me - helped me so much during the first part of the school term. Their support didn't stop but, unfortunately I became unwell. When I was at the children's home I'd experienced a bout of labyrinthitis, which is an infection in the inner ear that upsets the balance and makes a person dizzy. This returned and I had to take time off school as we entered the second half of the Autumn term.

In fact, I went and stayed with two dear Christian friends in Streatham for a few weeks as the labyrinthitis continued. I imagine that I was probably pretty low all round, both mentally and physically, because of the situation in the school - and it resulted in a slow return to health. I guess it wasn't very easy for my friends either, to have me there with my all round health not being very good! On my return to Homerton my doctor thought it would be best to wait and start back at school at the beginning of the Spring term in the January.

In some respects that time is, to be honest, a bit of a blur in places.... I'm sure I would have gone home to my parents for Christmas - but have absolutely no recollection of it at all.

Returning to School

January came and I duly returned to school and I found no adjustments at all re the fact that I'd been off on sick leave for half a term. The Headteacher continued to more or less let me get on with it as best I could on my own without any help or advice. You don't need to be a rocket scientist to guess that I didn't last for very long!! I think I was back in school for little more than a week before I ended up back at the doctors!

To be honest I don't think they were too sure what was wrong me, other than that the dizziness, etc persisted. I was told by the doctor that he thought I'd have to rethink what I wanted to do as he couldn't advise me to continue teaching..... Wow! My thinking from a natural point of view, remembering that there was little done about mental illness 50 years ago, is that he was out of his depth. I think that it was an accumulation of things - the dizziness, the inability to cope in the school situation, the shame from not being able to..... and possibly more! But I kept pushing it all down and not facing it - so it's not really surprising that it all eventually blew up!

So I found myself off school again and, from the doctor's point of view, unlikely to go back. I think it was possibly around that time that I started feeling sick in my stomach - and it didn't seem to want to go away. A friend I knew came and stayed with me that last weekend I spent in my little studio flat. I knew her from the BMMF Children's camps that I'd helped on and we'd become good friends. But, as usual by then, I did my covering up act (which I was pretty good at) and she didn't realise fully what was going on. Actually, we did speak about it years later and she told me that she'd known things weren't too good, but had no idea just how bad and how down I was, bless her.

It was on the Monday evening, after the weekend my friend had been staying with me, that my suicide attempt took place - which I have shared in chapter one - when 'God stepped in'.

My life had literally come to a standstill. According to the doctor I wouldn't be fit enough to teach, and if I didn't teach - what on earth was I going to do after spending three years training to do just that? We read in Proverbs 29:18 that "Without vision the people perish...." - and I think that was exactly what I was doing: perishing. I couldn't see any way out and, by that stage, felt I wasn't able to do anything else - but leave this earth. Obviously I wasn't thinking straight and, in fact by that stage, I don't believe I was thinking very much at all! What I was doing was a sin against God and what He teaches in His Word - but by then I couldn't even acknowledge that.

BUT GOD.... If you've read from the beginning of the book you know that it was at this point, when my life was at a complete standstill and as far as I was concerned was finished, that GOD stepped in and began to turn the tide - although I've still to share with you how it finally 'turned'!

As I write this now, I have a desire in my heart to pray for those who are reading this and thinking they've nothing left to live for. Believe me when I say you have everything to live for! You have a Heavenly Father who loves you and you are very precious to Him. It's never too late to begin your relationship with Him, if you haven't already; and if things have lapsed between you - He's always there to renew His relationship with you. He loves you to the extent that He let His only Son die on a cross at Calvary, the only motive being that we could be brought back into a living, loving relationship with Him.

3/2 Ebb and Flow and Returning to England

My Picture of the Sea

At this point I need to jump ahead somewhat, and explain how the analogy of the sea and the turning of the tide came into being and plays, what is really, a pivotal part in my story. And why the picture of the sea came to appear on the cover of this book!

In the early eighties I was living in a flat in Surbiton in Surrey which, in many ways, was virtually part of Kingston-upon-Thames. On my bedroom wall I had a picture of a sea rolling in on the shore and, one day when I was looking at it, I felt the Lord say to me that that was what He had done in my life. At the time I believed He meant that, just as the tide turned in the sea and flowed in a different direction, so He had stepped in and caused my life to flow in a different direction when He saved me from dying, back in the January of 1970. I admit that I didn't fully understand what He meant by that; stupidly didn't ask and, in fact, it's only more recently that I've begun to really grasp and understand it more.

At that time He also spoke to me about writing a book, to share what He had done in my life in order to help others. Now, that I did understand and it rather made me laugh, as it just seemed such an impossibility - and I knew I had absolutely no skill at writing! I did actually try and give it a go. This was way before mobile phones, laptops, tablets etc - and owning a computer was for the select few, and I wasn't one of them. So it was pen and paper for me - and I didn't get very far.....

As you've probably realised - that was the end of that, at that point, as far as I was concerned; although I had a very small seed thought that maybe, somewhere in the future.....? But maybe, as you might have already learned in your walk with the Lord, that it's not always wise to say 'never' to Him? After all, that's what I'd said when I was younger about working in an office, and especially about teaching - and what had I ended up doing.....?

Life at Ebb Tide

My understanding of the ebb tide is that the sea water on the shore, flows back out to sea until it reaches the lowest point - and that is where the ebb tide ends. I have already shared with you, in the first part of Chapter 3, how I felt my life had literally come to a standstill. My teaching career had, to all intents and purposes, been declared finished by the doctor and, both mentally and physically, I could see no way out.

I would add that, looking back now to that time, I realise that I was viewing myself only from the point of being what I 'did'. Now I would say that I'm 'me' - I'm who my Father made me to be, I'm not the 'job' that I do!

I feel the Lord has shown me that it was when I reached what was the ebb tide of my life, and feeling there was nothing more for me to live for - that was the exact time when He stepped in and saved me.

BUT - that was only the beginning of the turning of the tide.

The Flow of the Tide

When the ebb of the tide is reached - that's when the sea water begins to go back to shore. The amount of water increases as it flows back inland again. When the Lord showed me this, I began to realise that when He stepped in and saved me - that was the ebb and only the beginning....

Then came the equivalent of the flow back inland, that took me through to the time when the 'tide' completed its 'turning' in my life!

How did the Tide Turn?

Before I share with you how the tide finally turned - I need to remind you of something. At the end of Chapter 1, I said that, before I shared what happened when I returned to England with my parents, I would need to share some of the background that took me to the place where I needed God to step in - which is now completed. So here's what happened when we came back from Düsseldorf.

Arriving in Kineton, England

Where is Kineton you might ask? I think this was also probably my question when I first heard of it, and the possibility that we might be going there to live! Kineton is a village about 10 miles south of Warwick and is also where MOD Kineton is situated. We were in the position of having to do some house hunting - or at least my parents were!

My father, although a Fire Officer in the Army Fire Service was, in fact a civilian as the 'powers that be' civilianised the whole of the Army Fire Service, several years earlier, so that it came under the jurisdiction of the Civil Service rather than the Army. Whilst in Germany my parents were given an Army quarter, but when they returned to England they had to provide their own house. To be honest I don't remember the details of the intricacies of buying a house in Kineton - but it was a nice house with a reasonably sized garden, as my parents were keen gardeners.

I think I was probably concentrating more on what I should do work wise.... I was looking for teaching posts by this time. We had arrived back in June (at least I think it was about then!), and really I also needed something for the time between my arrival back in England and the start of the school term in September.

On the interim job front, I found a job working in Woolworths in Leamington Spa and think I caught a bus in each day as I had no transport of my own. At the same time I continued searching for schools near Kineton that needed a Religious Education teacher, or even Geography which had been my 'second' subject at college.

I started working at Woolworths but, unfortunately didn't last very long! I soon found that handling the money had the same affect on me as handling the tins in the NAAFI in Germany. I found myself having to give the job up and had to 'go on the dole' whilst I looked for another job.

Teaching Post

There didn't seem much around in the way of teaching posts that would be accessible to where I was living with my parents..... Then a vacancy came up in a girls' boarding school called Overstone, just outside Northampton. It was for a Residential Housemistress combined with a teaching post - based with the older girls of high school age.

There was also a junior section in the school - equivalent to the top two age years in a primary school. The teaching post itself was for teaching the Bible (Religious Education classes in fact) and Games lessons. I would have a flat in the main part of the school - the rooms where the classes were held were further up on the estate where the school was situated. I would be on duty upstairs in the morning and evening, overseeing the rising from and the departing to bed! The school Matron would also be on hand to help things run smoothly.

I obviously discussed the pros and cons of this post with my parents because of their request that, after what had happened, I would spend some time living at home until my life all round had become more stable.

But I find I'm jumping ahead of myself again.... a great deal happened prior to me getting to the stage of making a decision about the teaching vacancy at Overstone school!

My First Visit to South Chard Church.

My friend Wendy who had visited me when I was staying with Angela, after I first came out of hospital, invited me to go on holiday with her and another friend down to Chard in Somerset. Wendy's friend Doreen (not her flat mate, but another Doreen!) had taken her to the church at South Chard where the Holy Spirit was moving - and they were kind enough to invite me to join them. This was in August of 1970.

At one time Wendy had attended West Drayton Baptist Church and the minister at that time had been Andrew Jordan, whose wife was named Joy. At this time they were living in Chard and part of the Church at South Chard, and we were going to stay in their house, whilst they were away on holiday. On this, my first trip to Chard I didn't meet them, but am pleased to say that I did so on subsequent trips - in fact I think I stayed with them when I visited later in the year during the October half-term.

We had a wonderful holiday - good weather as we explored the area, one which I didn't know, and opportunity to make new friends at the church there! For me personally, it was a holiday I shall never forget and one that I have continued to thank the Lord for, all through the many years since then! At that first Sunday morning meeting I went to, the Lord started a work in my heart and life which is still going on.

I had been baptised in the Spirit whilst I was at teacher training college (1966 to 1969) and been blessed with the gift of speaking in tongues. I'd also been to meetings where the Holy Spirit was moving and the gifts operating. But that first meeting at South Chard was, for me personally, a whole different ball game! It was in and through the worship that the Spirit just got hold of me - to me it felt as though the 'knots' tied up tight on the inside of me after all that had happened were gradually starting to loosen as I joined in the praise and worship of the King of Kings. I don't really know how else to describe it!

That first week we explored the countryside and visited with people from South Chard Church that Doreen had become friends with during her visits there. The weather was good and it was lovely to relax in God's creation and be blessed fellowshipping with His people.

It amazes me at times how the Lord takes such care in not only preparing us for what He wants to do in our lives - but also goes to great length in preparing the scene where it's going to happen. And the way He makes sure He has all the other people there who will be involved as well. I find it so humbling that He cares for us so much that He makes sure of every detail that's needed to make it happen. I was so aware that He had taken such care of me and loved me so much to make sure that, after the 'ebb' tide, the 'flow' would happen and the tide would indeed finally turn in my life.

3/3 The Tide Finally Turns

The Flow of the Tide - God's Preparation

The experience I had in that first meeting I went to in the Church at South Chard, the one where I felt knots were being untied inside me - was, I believe, one of the ways the Lord prepared me for the tide finally turning. And we were so blessed by the fellowship with people from the church through those days; it felt that we were being wrapped up in God's love.

It never occurred to me that my Father was preparing me for what He wanted to do in me at the end of that first week. I suppose it's really only now that I realise how He had had all those months planned out and knew exactly what He was doing! Those months, from when He stepped in during January '70 - right through to completing the turn of the tide in the August. And He even took me out of the country to get me on my own, so He could form a relationship with me in a new way!

And I never realised at the time how He actually got everything sorted out, concerning my living and teaching again, so that when the tide finally turned - all was set, ready for me to move forward and live the new life He wanted for me. Everything was prepared.....

The Tide is Finally Turned

So how and what actually happened to 'finally turn the tide', after all those months since the 'ebb tide' in my life and, in some ways even more important, what was the outcome? And what affect did it have on my life going forward? I will endeavour to share the answers to these questions with you and, as I continue to share my story, the impact it has had on my life through the following years.

We were about to enter our second week; it was Friday night and we'd been on holiday in South Chard since the previous Saturday. Before we had our tea I had stood and looked in the mirror hanging over the fireplace, and I'd found myself transported back to that night of January 20 that I'd attempted the suicide. For some reason, after I'd taken all the Anadin and before turning the gas on and sticking my head in the oven, I'd looked into my eyes in the mirror and realised they portrayed something pretty awful.....

It's literally only as I've been writing this that I've realised that what I was actually doing was looking into the pit that the enemy had prepared for me - and I believe that that was what was being reflected in my eyes. What the enemy somehow hadn't reckoned on, was the fact that there was One far greater that was also there - and He would protect me!

In the intervening months I don't ever recall looking into my eyes in the same way, although obviously I must have looked in a mirror on a regular basis - but I never saw that same look again! Not until that Friday night - and there was no way I was going to say anything!! We had our tea in front of the fire on our laps - baked beans on toast!! Only I was having great difficulty eating mine and just couldn't finish it..... I guess the others began to realise something was wrong and asked me - but I didn't seem to be able to get any words out and, as time passed things got worse and I could feel myself sinking – I don't know how else to describe it!

I think that eventually I tried to open my mouth to try and explain - but all that actually happened was that I erupted into tears and sobs that just got worst as time passed and there seemed no way to stop them!! I guess the others were praying and asking the Lord what to do and eventually Doreen suggested she contacted someone called Tony Nash - part of the Church. She apparently knew him quite well - she would have needed to, because I think by then it was after midnight.... What actually happened in the end was, they bundled me into the car and drove to Tony's house in Chard and Doreen finally managed to make contact with him!

I really have little recollection of that journey, although I vaguely remember waiting in the car, I guess with Wendy, in an empty street - presumably while Doreen made contact with Tony..... And I don't think I remember anything about the journey down to the church - only that somehow I was sitting in a soundproofed room (which I only found out later). The sobbing was subsiding a bit by the time we got into the room..... and I sat on a chair, or rather it was nearer to huddling on the chair with my head as low as I could get it!

One of the first things Tony said to me was that I should 'sit up' and 'look up' and my goodness the lesson I learned in doing that has stayed with me all these years - the release it brought in me by doing what he said was incredible, it started me on the road out of what I was immersed in! Tony also took my arms and held them right up as he prayed for me.... I think he prayed in English as well as in tongues but I couldn't begin to tell you what he prayed!

However, I can tell you about the picture which the Lord gave to me, and what He said about it.... The picture was very simple. It was a signpost at a crossroads with, as you might guess, two ways to go!! And I realised that it was me who was at a crossroads! And that was it. I couldn't see any indication on the signs as to where the two ways led to. But, somehow, I knew exactly where both of them led. With what I know now, I would say that I knew in my spirit exactly where each road would lead me.

I believe that what the Lord was saying to me about where those two signs were pointing was this: .....the first road would lead me to a psychiatric institution. Given that this was 1970, it would have still been the old style restricted mental institution and health care that was still in operation at that time. I was under no illusion, and somehow knew that once there it would have been as a long term patient, without any hope of coming out again.

.....the second road would lead me back to the fullness of life in Jesus, and all He had planned for me in the life He was giving back to me. That actually was what He was in fact doing - giving me my life. And with it, a relationship with Him that was somehow different to the one I had known before - the life that had brought me to the point where I attempted suicide.

From the picture the Lord gave me, and what He said to my

heart and spirit, I realised, and was in no doubt, that I was faced with a definite choice to make. I also knew that it was definitely my choice to make - not a choice that the Lord would make for me.....

I believe that the choice I was confronted with, through the picture the Lord gave me involving the crossroads, would be the culmination of the 'turning of the tide' - after He had stepped in and brought me back from the 'ebb'.

If my choice was the one that ultimately ended me up in the psychiatric institution - that would take me right back and leave me in the endless 'ebb and flow' of emotions and needing long term medical help.

BUT - by taking that step forward along the second road, I believe the Lord 'turned the tide' in my life for good. It was through following that road that my Father has brought me back into the fullness of relationship with Him. It was through 'turning the tide' that He has led me into all He has taken me through in my life since then, and played such an important part in bringing me to where I am now in my relationship with Him today.

It's important to never discount the experiences that the Lord takes you through - even though, at the time they happen, there may not be an obvious reason or outcome. It is so important to keep your heart and your spirit open to all that the Holy Spirit wants to show you, even though it might not be revealed until a later date. And also to learn what He shows you along the way..... for example: when Tony made me lift my head up, and then lifted my arms up - it brought such release in my spirit and helped me

receive from the Lord. It's something I've shared with others and encouraged them to do - and seen the Lord bring them release. That's why I say to never discount any experience Father takes you through!

Going Forward After the Tide had Turned

I realise that I was a very different person going into the second week of our holiday - seeing everything through completely different eyes. When we left to head home, I took with me the name and address of a couple with connections to South Chard, who lived in Dunchurch, not far from Rugby. It was also not far from Kineton and on the Friday I got back I wrote them a letter and got it into the post straight away.... I explained who I was and how I came to be writing to them - Dennis and Pam King. I shared that I'd just come back from South Chard and was believing that at some point, in God's timing, I hoped to join with them in the meeting they had in their home - the House Church that South Chard had told me about.

Well.... sometimes, the Lord moves things along very quickly! Late afternoon on the Saturday the door bell rang at my parents' house in Kineton. The gentleman standing there said he was on his way to the Saturday night meeting in Dunchurch - would I like to go, explaining that Den and Pam had rung him and asked if he could call in and ask me on the way. Wow! Believe me, I was pretty well speechless!! Would I like to go? I certainly would! In fact, I went then and again the next day for the Sunday meetings as well. On Sunday there was an afternoon meeting; then we had tea together and those who were able to stay, met in the evening as well.

I don't remember very much about the Saturday evening meeting, but something happened in the Sunday afternoon meeting that has remained with me ever since. There was a lady sitting more or less opposite me in the room where we were meeting. The meeting began and we were praising and worshipping the Lord and here, like the meetings in South Chard, there were no screens or anything like that with words on..... We learned the words of the songs as we sang them - many of them short and many of them based on Bible verses - and the power of the Holy Spirit helped everyone.

But - back to what I wanted to share about the lady sitting across from me.... There was something about the 'light' in her face that was different and particularly so as we worshipped. As she worshipped, her obvious love for Jesus was almost palpable and all I could do initially was watch her - and there grew in me a desire to love Jesus in the way that she loved Him. I was introduced to this lady after the meeting - her name was Jean and her husband's name was Peter. The three of us in due course became close friends, and you'll see how this came about as I continue to share my story through this time.

God had done it again..... He had sorted all the problems out - including the one the doctor in Hackney had come up with concerning me having to give up teaching because of my health! To my knowledge, it was never spoken of again. Always remember that God has a plan for your life and that He sees and is leading you in line with His whole plan - not just the part that you're currently aware of. And all the time He prepares you, in

your present circumstances, for what He has planned for you in the next steps that you'll be following.

Start of a New Season

With the tide having finally turned, I was very much setting out into a new season of my life. And the contacts had been made regarding fellowship within the Body of Christ, when I was put in contact with the fellowship at Dunchurch. One more step to take now….. starting to teach again!

Yes, after discussing the whole situation with my parents - they agreed that they thought it would be good for me to apply for the post at Overstone School. I sent in my application for the post - and was accepted to start at the beginning of the autumn term.

So, there I was - a new church family, plus a new teaching post. All set to move into the new season and the new life that my Father had planned and sorted out for me!

God is so, so good how He plans everything in love for us!

CHAPTER 4

God's Training

4/1 Teaching Again and God's Training Begins

Starting to Teach Again

Having talked it all through with my parents they agreed that it made sense for me to accept the vacancy I'd been offered at Overstone School. With it being very near to Northampton, it wasn't actually very far away from them in Kineton. After all that had happened during my first year out of college it was, in fact, an ideal teaching position to get me adjusted and into a career of teaching. The other amazing thing about me teaching at Overstone School was that it was here that I first came to help with the BMMF Children summer camps. Yes, this was where I was first involved in Christian outreach - how amazing is that!

Overstone School

In my position as Housemistress, I obviously didn't follow a normal work pattern of a teacher. My main block of time off was one complete day each week and this happened on a Tuesday. You can imagine my delight, and how I thanked the Lord, when I found out that it was on a Tuesday evening that Peter and Jean, the couple I had met at Dunchurch, held a mid week meeting in their home in Daventry. It always thrills me the way the Lord arranges things so wonderfully.

Once I had started the term at Overstone School, I started travelling over to Daventry on a Tuesday on a regular basis. I went over initially by bus and spent most of the day there and stayed for the evening meeting - then Peter very kindly took me back to the school afterwards. I realised I needed to get myself some form of transport and got myself a Vespa scooter - and that gave me the freedom I needed! I also restarted driving lessons, which I had begun when in London but which had, for obvious reasons, come to rather an abrupt end; and, optimistically began looking around to see if I could buy myself a small car.

For the first time I found myself being challenged to move out in an area completely alien to me. I felt the Lord was moving me towards a car that I didn't have the money for - and that I was to trust Him to work it out. It was a red mini being sold by the garage not far from the school for £145, which back in early 1971 seemed a great deal of money - especially when I didn't have it. The biggest challenge of all was that I believed I was to go to the chap at the garage and tell him that I believed the Lord wanted me to buy the car - but I hadn't got the money. I mean, how ridiculous was that? I felt a fool just thinking about it!

The trouble was, I lost my peace and didn't regain it until I agreed to do it.... I'll never forget the day that I said "yes" and planned to go to the garage after morning lessons were over. Imagine my surprise, plus the sick feeling in my stomach, when in the morning break I walked out of the classroom into the courtyard - and there was the chap from the garage, who'd come up to the school to see someone. I could hardly believe my eyes, but realised the Lord meant me to do business! I have no real idea what I actually said to him - my only recollection is that it was somewhat garbled to say the least of it.

However, amazingly he seemed to somehow understand what I was saying to him - and suggested I go down to the garage after morning lessons and we could talk about it. The upshot of it was..... he set up a plan for me to buy the car over a period of six months, and proceeded to do all the paperwork needed to make me a very proud owner of a little red mini! The headmaster at the school gave me permission to drive within the grounds of the school. This was a great help, as I failed my first test on the driving school's car but, with the extra practice and taking the test a month later in my own car - I passed.

Hallelujah!

And what happened to the scooter, you will probably ask.... The Lord had already spoken to me about giving it to Barbara - also living in Daventry and close friends with Peter and Jean, who, by this time, was also a friend of mine.

Those early days of learning on my weekly visits to Daventry - I look back on as the beginning of my training in so many ways. I would often sit with Jean and Barbara and listen to them sharing the Word and sharing how the Lord was speaking to them and dealing with things in their lives. I say 'listen' because it was my first real experience of learning how to fellowship in the Body of Christ and I wasn't used to saying much - but boy, did I drink it all in!

I believe those days were the beginning of what I call my 'training' and I will share more as my story unfolds. But I would like to encourage you to learn as much as you can from the people in your Christian community who the Lord has placed you with. Initially it might be to listen, as it was with me, but as time goes on and you put into operation in your lives what you are learning - you'll begin to realise how you are growing in your walk with the Lord and you'll start to also share. Sometimes they appear to be small steps - but, whatever the size of the steps, they'll always take you forward.

New Horizons

During the Easter Holidays a group of us from the fellowship at Dunchurch, travelled over to Ipswich to the Easter Convention there, that at that time was held each year by the Good News Crusade - led by Don Double. It was quite a gathering and we were all blessed during our time there and it was lovely to be together as a group. It was the start of something new in my life - although I never realised it on that first visit.

I enjoyed my time teaching and being at Overstone, but I'd begun to realise that I was somewhat tied down by the hours I worked there, due to my position as Housemistress. I think I began to realise that, in my heart I wanted more involvement with the Christian community that the Lord had placed me with - the folk at Dunchurch, and even more so the smaller group in Daventry. Basically, I had a growing hunger to learn more about going deeper in my relationship with the Lord, and had begun to feel a bit restricted.

We had a copy of Tes (the paper advertising teaching posts) delivered to our staff room each week, and over the weeks I'd begun to browse through it again - much as I had when I was in Germany. After we started back to school after the Easter break, I came across an advertisement for a Religious Education teaching assistant in Daventry Comprehensive School. I didn't take much persuading to get an application form and apply for the post!

With the Whitson weekend approaching and half-term coming up, there were plans afoot for us all to go to Ipswich again! This time it was actually a weekend conference being held at a school at Woodbridge, just outside of Ipswich. It was organised by a lady called Freda Flude who had actually been involved with Don Double who organised the Easter Convention. She had been pointed out to me, but I hadn't actually met her at that point. The speaker over the weekend was Harry Greenwood - a minister who was actually based in South Chard, although previously he had worked with Don Double. He had stayed with Freda previously when attending the Easter Convention - and they had become firm friends.

We took camping equipment with us this time round, as we would be sleeping in the classrooms upstairs. The women and children together, and the men folk together. Meals would be cooked in the school kitchens. Needless to say it was great fun being altogether but, even more than that, we were all so blessed by Harry's ministry and the opportunity to worship and fellowship together. One memory that stands out is what happened after the evening meeting on the Saturday night. We went off to bed, having been blessed in a wonderfully free time of worship but, after putting on our night attire, we had such a desire to go on worshipping the Lord - that we ended up back downstairs and continued worshipping into the early hours!

The other memory that I won't forget, came about through a conversation I had with a lady called Greta, who was from Rugby and part of the fellowship at Dunchurch. I'd been sharing with her about the application that I'd made for the teaching post in Daventry. She listened closely to what I shared and then said very firmly "I believe the job is yours". It certainly took me by surprise - and, actually, it obviously took her by surprise as she quickly put her hand over her mouth and I realised from the expression on her face that she'd had no intention of saying that. But, by then it was too late - she'd said it! It really hit me in my spirit and I said to her that I believed that it was a word from the Lord for me to take hold of.

I have to say that this was the first time that I'd experienced what I felt was such a clear word from the Lord in this way! It dropped into my spirit - and there it stayed.... and you'll see what the Lord did with it as I share with you in due course. Never

ignore it when the Lord speaks to you through the Holy Spirit. If it's something He is giving you a nudge on to do in your current situation - then do it! Sometimes, as it was for me in this situation, if it's about something in the future - grasp and hold it in your spirit until He shows you the next step! If it's something you're not sure on - begin to move towards it and ask the Lord to show you if you've got it wrong. Remember the Lord can't move you into something new if you're stationery. You need to start to move.... even if initially it's in the wrong direction - if you're on the move the Lord can direct you!

A Time of Waiting

School carried on in much the same way, and I continued spending my Tuesdays in Daventry - and drove over to Dunchurch whenever I could on a Sunday afternoon and evening. And I waited! I waited to hear news of the job at the school in Daventry. I was still convinced that it was where the Lord wanted me to be - but I didn't hear a thing. Absolutely nothing! As I shared earlier, this was a new experience for me - so sure that this job was for me, but nothing happening to confirm what I was believing for. I kept praying, and there were days when the enemy very nearly convinced me that I was imagining it all - but by God's grace I held on.

As always - time stops for no one; and it got towards the end of term and I still hadn't heard anything. I'm not sure now whether it was a couple of Tuesdays before the end of term, or the final one of term - but as this particular Tuesday approached, I began to get this thought that maybe I should go into the school and ask what was happening. I felt somewhat sick at the thought of it, knowing you don't normally enquire about a teaching post in this manner! But I couldn't stop thinking that this is what I should do.....

I drove over to the senior part of the school - the premises were in two places and the Headmaster's office was in the upper part of the school. I found my way to the school secretary's office and explained, very hesitatingly I might add, that in the early part of the term I had applied for the RE teaching post that had been advertised, and that I wondered if there was any news on the outcome. Amazingly she didn't send me packing, but sat me down whilst she went and spoke to the Head. Whew! One step taken!

I waited for a while, and then she came out and said the Head would see me - and showed me into his office. It was very strange really, because he was sitting at his desk with a big pile of papers in front of him - which I suddenly realised were application forms. He was, in fact, working his way through them and didn't even look up as he began to speak to me! He explained that the original advertisement I'd responded to never came to anything, as the person who was leaving and creating the vacancy - decided not to. But - and this was when my spirit did a sort of somersault in me - the day before (on the Monday) the person had changed their mind and had decided to finish after all.

The Head was intent on looking through the original application forms, to find the one I had sent - in order to have another look at it. He found it and then, to my utter amazement, began to interview me for the post - decided he would like to have me on the teaching staff - and offered me the vacancy on the spot!

From there he went on to explain that Daventry council, to encourage people to come and teach in the town, were also offering new teachers a council flat if they wanted to live locally. I found myself, within what was probably only about roughly an hour in time - in possession of a new teaching post, plus a flat to live in. The icing on the cake was that my new home turned out to be about 5 to 10 mins away from where my friends Peter and Jean lived with their four daughters; and roughly the same distance from where Barbara lived.

Have you ever felt blown away at what the Lord has done in your life? That's the only way I can describe how I felt when I walked out of the school that day in the possession of not only a new job, but also a new home! Hallelujah! And, even just sharing this with you today, I'm excited when I remember what the Lord did. All that time I was believing the Lord for a teaching post in that school - there actually wasn't one there.... In fact, it was only the day before the Lord took me into the school to ask about it - that it had actually materialised! How amazing is that!

As you walk forward with the Lord under the guidance of the Holy Spirit - never underestimate what He is able to do in your life, if you are willing to listen. But also remember that, just as He works in the 'big' moments in your life - He wants to work in just the same way in the 'small' moments. Those times when He does things for you that only you and He know about. Those times He sorts and straightens things out for you that are just between the two of you. They can be just as precious in your relationship as the more momentous occasions.

I look back to my year at Overstone and believe that that was when the Lord began to teach and train me in a way I had never experienced before. Each one of us, that's you and me included, need to trust that our Father will help us learn how to walk in harmony with Him. We need to learn to walk with Him in our own relationship - just the two of us. But we also need to learn to walk with others in the Body of Christ in a relationship in which can learn from each other. We don't necessarily need to have that learning/training relationship with many. But we do need to trust the Lord to place us with those who have more experience than ourselves - so we are challenged and can grow. I want to ask you if you have those sort of people around you, that you can identify as ones the Lord has placed you in fellowship with so that you can grow? They may change over time because we go through seasons when Father puts us with different ones to teach us what we need to know.

But if you are unable to make that identification amongst those you have contact with.... I challenge you to ask the Lord to bring them into your life and identify them to you. And be prepared for the fact He might remove others to make way for the people you need!

4/2 God's Training Continues in Daventry

Moving to Daventry

Well, I had a new job, a new home and time to sort it out through the summer holiday before I started at the school in Daventry in the September. What I didn't have - was very much to put in the flat.....!! My friends in Daventry and Dunchurch rallied round and helped as much as possible, but I needed some money to get some of the bigger items such as furniture. I knew my friends were praying, as was I, and asking the Lord to provide me with what I needed. I think initially I moved in with the few things I did have - sort of half camping, and trusting the Lord in it all.

I remember taking a trip down to London to visit my friends Wendy and Doreen in their flat in Streatham and on the return journey being very tired and arriving back at my flat very late - possibly in the early hours even. Let's put it this way - I wasn't what I would call very with it! I had some post waiting for me, one of them a small brown envelope. When I opened it there was a cheque made out to me, but no explanation as to who it was from or what it was for - and then I suddenly realised it was a gift and would help me get something for the flat. I thought it was a cheque for £20 - which, back in the summer of '71, was a fair amount of money.

The thing was, I was so tired I couldn't really work out the number of naughts on it. And then I suddenly realised that there were too many naughts for it to be £20, and was in fact a cheque for £200 - quite a sizeable sum! Wow! Another first for me - I had never experienced a gift of money in this way before, and I was sure it was a gift from my Father, and such an answer to prayer. As you can imagine I was thrilled at the way the Lord provided me with that money and helped set me up with all the basics that I needed to be comfortable in the new home He had given to me. By the time term started I was settled in and ready to embark on the new season He was taking me into.

Don't ever underestimate God's ability to provide you with all you need. Especially don't assume that He's only interested in your spiritual well being and growth. He desires to provide you with ALL you need in the whole of your life and that applies just as much to all the practical things you need as well. He tells us very clearly in His Word to ask Him for all we need - and He will answer.

A New Season

It didn't take me long to begin to realise why the Lord had moved me out of Overstone and into Daventry! You see, whilst I was at Overstone I only saw my friends regularly on a Tuesday, and folk over in Dunchurch, when I could get there..... Once I was living in Daventry I was able to go over to the meetings in Dunchurch - on a Saturday evening, and Sunday afternoon and evening - on a regular basis. And I was able to see my friends locally as much as I wanted to, apart from when I was at work, as well as being there for the Tuesday mid week meeting in Peter and Jean's home.

As time went by, I became pretty much a member of Peter and Jean's extended family. Bless them - they were so gracious in including me in their lives, and I was so grateful to them and to the Lord for bringing it about. It was the first time that I had lived on my own, as the short time I'd spent on my own in Homerton couldn't really be counted. Having come from a largish family, there were five of us children, I wasn't that used to being on my own. And I have to admit that, although a lot had happened already in my life, I was still relatively young in my walk with the Lord and knew I had so much more to learn! I also believe that at that stage I was, in many ways, too dependent on other people at times.

I shared previously how I had initially begun to learn to fellowship and start to share what the Lord was doing and saying in my life, as I spent time with Jean and Barbara on those Tuesday afternoons when I came over from Overstone. Now, in just the same way, I was learning through me spending time with this new family Father had placed me in. Peter and Jean had a very stable and strong relationship with the Lord and with each other - and within that relationship they always pointed others in His direction, never towards themselves. In fact I remember Jean saying if she thought anyone might be getting too dependent on her in any way, and it's stayed with me all these years - she would say very clearly and concisely that if they started depending on her the Lord would make sure she let them down, because she knew her feet were 'made of clay'......

We all need these sort of people in our lives - those who will always point us in the direction of Jesus and make sure we don't

become in any way dependent on them. I am so thankful that the Lord showed me this in those early days of what I call 'training' and I've continued through the years to ask Him to keep me alert not to let it happen. I have to confess there have been times when I came close - and He's had to stop me and show me what was happening and deal with it. You may find this happening to you but if the Lord shows you then do something to correct it, and thank Him for highlighting it to you. He does it because He loves you and He's the one who wants your whole heart - not just part of it. It will make you stronger. And, if you don't have people already in your life that always point you in His direction, then ask Him to somehow bring them to you!

Days of Training

I can think of two specific instances, in those early days in Daventry, where the Lord used Jean to point out things He wanted to teach me! The first happened in the first term of teaching at the new school I was at. Remember this was, in effect, my first 'run' at being at what I would call a 'normal' school - that's if any school can be called normal! My time at the school in the East End of London wasn't anywhere near to it - and teaching in a private boarding school is completely different to a state run day school..... I think I was a bit overwhelmed with all the adjustments of moving to the flat and starting a new teaching position and, all round, adjusting to a different way of life.

Possibly it was the result of a particular difficulty within school, I can't exactly pinpoint the reason - but I do remember this particular morning when I woke but didn't want to get up, and certainly didn't want to go to school. So I snuggled down in the safety of my bed - and stayed there, trying to shut out the thoughts of what the results might be! Then there was a banging on my front door and, when I eventually opened it - there was Jean, come to find out what was wrong. I didn't possess a telephone and it was long before mobile phones - so the only way of contacting me was to come to the flat.

I can't remember quite how she had found out - but she had come! We talked through what had happened and why - and she gently pointed out, what I already knew if I'd been honest with myself and the Lord, that if I was facing difficulties this wasn't the way of coping with it. I needed to ask the Lord to help me face up to whatever I needed to, trust Him to help me - and get myself dressed and into school.

Another lesson underlined.... You would have thought I would have well and truly learned it when I ended up attempting suicide. What I did begin to learn more about was the fact we often need to be faced with similar lessons - and each time we come through them, the Lord takes us into a deeper place of learning which results in being in a greater place of strength.

The second instance was in connection with my driving. We met together for worship and fellowship in Dunchurch in the afternoon on a Sunday; had tea together and, those who were able to, stayed on for further fellowship in the evening. Those with younger children sometimes took them home after tea so they weren't too late because of school next day. Sometimes I would take Jean home with her youngest daughter, so Peter could stay on for the evening with their older girls.

This particular Sunday we got back to Jean's home, Joanna went in, and Jean stayed to talk to me before I went on back to my flat. Jean asked me straight out what was bothering me - she was always direct about things and I appreciated that. When I asked her what she meant, she said she knew that when I'm not at peace my driving gets a bit erratic - and it seemed to be at that time..... I said I wasn't aware of anything, but would talk to the Lord about it and get back to her. And I knew that she would be praying for me to get it sorted.

Well, you might know that, when I was willing to face up to something not being right (when Jean had asked me the question I began to realise that she was right about my driving) - the Lord began to show me. I began to realise that, although it wasn't deliberate, I was spending as little time as possible at the flat - and was off out visiting people whenever I could. I had to acknowledge to my self, and to the Lord (though He obviously was aware all along) that I found it difficult to be at the flat on my own - it was much easier to be out spending time elsewhere. As I talked it over with the Lord, I came to see that I needed to come to a place of really believing and trusting what He says in His Word - that He is always with me and that I'm never alone.

It was such a relief when Father showed me what was at the root of my lack of peace. I somehow knew in my spirit that, with Him revealing the truth to me, I could trust Him to lead me through to the place of resting in it and living in it day by day. I realised too that it was another step towards a deeper relationship with Him.

How do you get on when you're on your own - do you live on

your own and find it lonely and difficult? Go to the Word and remind yourself what your Father says about being on your own - that, in fact you're not! Jesus is living in you by the power of the Holy Spirit and therefore you are never actually alone. But, the enemy will do his utmost to convince you that you are - be aware that it's something you, and me, has to go on learning. It's not a done deal in one go - we have to go on reminding ourselves and standing in the truth of it - the Holy Spirit is the One to help us. So call on Him!

Learning to Forgive

As a Christian I obviously knew something about what was taught in the Word concerning the subject of forgiveness. I'm ashamed to admit that I think it was more head knowledge, than anything in the way of actual experience. I think it was fairly early on during those years in Daventry that I went to a meeting not that far away, although not connected to where I went on a regular basis to Dunchurch. I don't remember very much about the meeting other than that there was freedom in the worship and life in the ministry. I'm not even sure of the main subject of the speaker - but, what did hit home in my spirit, was when he began speaking about our need to forgive one another.

He emphasised the need of this even, and in fact especially, if we knew the other person(s) was in the wrong. Given that it must have been more than a year, and possibly nearer two years, since I'd left the school in London - you can imagine my surprise when thoughts of the Headteacher came flooding back to me. I remembered my hurt and anger at the position she'd placed me in, with very little help. It was such a shock when the Lord started to speak to me about forgiving her..... and I realised that it was the last thing I wanted to do!

However, by then I was beginning to learn that, when Father spoke to me like this, I really did need to take notice and do something about it. I was learning that if I ignored the nudge of the Holy Spirit, which is what was happening, then it would hold me back from going on with the Lord. Plus I'd found that He would keep taking me 'round the mountain' until I was obedient and did what He'd asked me. Unfortunately I have to confess that I'm not always very quick at acting, but I do know what a relief it is when I eventually do....

In this instance I responded pretty rapidly, realising it would be such a blockage to me going on if I ignored it. There and then in the meeting I forgave the Headteacher in my heart and asked the Lord to help me mean it and show me anything else I needed to do. I may well have actually raised my hand in acknowledgement, but my memory isn't completely clear and certain on that. I returned home after the meeting with a determination in my heart to hold onto what I'd said to the Lord, and I realised also that there was something else I needed to do. I wrote a letter to the Headteacher explaining how I had felt about it all and her part in it - and asked her to forgive me. I don't know if she ever received the letter or not, as I never heard from her. But I was at peace that I'd been obedient to what the Lord had shown me to do.

I would love to be able to say that, me forgiving the Headteacher, was the start of me learning much more about forgiveness - but have to be honest that my learning experience in that area did not grow as much as it should have done through the years. But I am pleased to be able to share with you that it's an area that the Lord has been dealing with me and teaching me more about, in more recent years. I hope to share more with you when I reach that stage of my story.

I can't stress enough the importance of our forgiving others for what they may have done, and in some cases still are doing, to us or to those we love. Do you have difficulties, or have had in the past, forgiving people? Actually, and it's taken me quite some time to learn this, the difficulty we have is in realising the fact that we are the ones who get most hurt when we're unwilling to forgive. It's us, you and me, who suffer the most. It's only in forgiving, that we are actually freed from the situation and it stops affecting our lives through the pain, guilt, anger and any other emotion involved. I'm not saying it's easy but, with the help that the Lord is more than willing to give us - it sets us free!

A New Family

I said earlier that I felt that I became a part of Peter and Jean's family during my time in Daventry and I look back at that season in my life as very much a time of training. I saw them most days, and learned so much through seeing them live their life as a family with Jesus always central to what was happening in their lives. This applied to their attitude to one another and to all those they were in contact with. When difficulties arose with their children I saw how they would sit down as a family and talk things through and pray and seek the Lord's help in the outcome.

It's a time when I began to learn more about how our attitude affects the outcome of the situations we find ourselves in. And, most important of all I believe, I began to learn and understand more about praising God in all that's happening in our lives on a day to day basis - not just when we gather with other believers in a meeting. I could see the difference it made in the way Peter and Jean lived their lives, when they always had thanks and praise on their lips - whether they felt like it or not. In Psalm 34:1 it says "I WILL bless the Lord at all times; His praise shall continually be in my mouth." David encourages us to do this - he found it worked and wanted others to know as well.

Through the years I have always been so grateful to the Lord in placing me there to learn more - I believe it gave me a firm foundation to move forward in my life. Some of what I learned I didn't even realise at the time - only in later years when certain situations arose, and I found I'd coped with them and traced it back to what I had learned at that time! Also during that time, and mainly through the contacts of those I was 'doing life' with (for want of a better expression) I was given the opportunity to meet others in the wider family of God. Many of them who also played a part in my life through the following years - and I will share more about how that came to be in the next section.

What sort of foundation is your walk with the Lord built on? Are you conscious of having those around you in the Body, whom you have seen as examples on the way to help you grow in your relationship with the Lord? If that hasn't been the case, have you been challenged to find out in other ways - for example direct from the Word and trusted the Holy Spirit to teach you? Or, do you feel as though you need to know more in that area - but aren't sure how to go about it? I would encourage you to ask the Lord to direct you towards someone who could maybe act as a mentor and disciple you. If you think about it - that's what Jesus did with His disciples, and it's what we all need in one way or another for us to grow in our walk and relationship with the Lord.

4/3 Wider Contacts in God's Family

Meeting up with More of God's Family

In the time I lived in Daventry and, actually it also applies to the year before that when I was teaching at Overstone - I began to have the opportunity to have contact with members of God's wider Family.

I think my first visit to South Chard (see Ch 3/3), just prior to starting teaching at Overstone, was what I would call my first contact. And what a contact that was when the ***rolling tide*** in my life, which had started when God stepped in and saved me, ***finally turned*** when He presented me with the pivotal choice at the crossroads - and I made the choice to go forward into all He had planned for my life! Those two weeks I spent there and all that happened with God ***turning the tide***, which would in fact affect the rest of my life - gave South Chard a very special place in my heart which has continued through the years to the present day.

I have visited through the years, often stayed at the Manor in the early days with Uncle Sid and Aunty Mill, and currently have fairly regular contact as I live not too far away. During my time in Daventry in the early seventies - a group of us from the fellowship went on holiday to the West Country. We spent a week down in Cornwall followed by a week at South Chard - and what a blessed time we had together! Actually many of the contacts with other parts of the Family made in the following years, came about through that initial contact - the first one being my introduction to the fellowship at Dunchurch, which included meeting Peter and Jean, so instrumental in my life in the following years.

There followed my first visit to the Ipswich Convention and my initial meeting with Don Double and the Good News Crusade, and subsequently Freda Flude - when she arranged the weekend at Woodbridge school where I met Harry Greenwood (from South Chard), along with others who were actually based in the Ipswich area. One of them was Jenny Reid, an Irish girl living with Freda at that time, who the Lord brought into my life at a later date - but I'm once again jumping ahead of my story.

Can you see how the Lord weaves individual people into our lives - placing us in situations where we make contact with them, although it may be years later when He uses them in teaching us certain things that He wants us to learn? I look back now, through the years, and am amazed at how He put me in contact with people in the Family at different times who, in a later season (and sometimes more than one season), played a big part in my life. But I'm so thankful and grateful that He did.

The Ipswich Convention

I shared earlier about how a group of us from Dunchurch Fellowship went to a Convention in Ipswich at the Easter of 1971, which was held by Don Double and the Good News Crusade. After that first visit I remember us going the three following years - and getting to know a fair number of folk in Ipswich as well. One of the years a few of us stayed with Muriel and her family in Felixstowe, down on the coast. She was part of the Fellowship, meeting at Freda's house in Ipswich - known to us affectionately as '413'! We remained friends for many years, in fact until the Lord took her home just over 30 years later. Another year a group of us stayed on a caravan site down at Felixstowe, and catered for ourselves. That year we also had friends from a church in Leicester who came to the convention with us - yet another expansion of God's Family!

There were various men of God who came and ministered at the convention each year. I want to share with you in particular, about the final year I went to Ipswich for the convention, which was 1974, as it had a significant impact on my life. Bryn Jones was the main speaker, and I have to confess that, nearly fifty years later, I'm not able to recount a great deal of his ministry that year! However, I am able to share a small part of the ministry in one of the morning meetings - and what resulted from it....

I don't recall the overall subject of his message that morning - but part of it was based on Matthew 14:22-33, when the disciples were in a boat and a storm rose up. Jesus walked on the water and approached the boat they were in - they screamed with fright, and He told them to take courage and to stop being afraid. Peter said to Jesus, if it really was Him, to tell him (Peter) to walk on the water to Him - and Peter got out of the boat and walked towards Him, when He said "Come!" But, when Peter saw and felt the strong wind, he was frightened and began to sink and called out for help to the Lord. Jesus helped him and when they got into the boat - the wind stopped.

Bryn said that many of us are like Peter, wanting to get out of the 'boat' (situation) we're in - but then losing our trust in what the Lord wants us to do and, instead of standing in what He has said, we slip and fall and so often Father has to rescue us. We should only get out of the boat when He says, and then we need to stand firmly in what He shows us to do. Bryn went on to say that there was at least one person in the meeting, maybe more, that the Lord was saying to them that it was their time to get out of the boat - and he wanted to pray for them.

Well, I'd known as soon as Bryn had started speaking about Peter getting out of the boat, that the Lord was speaking to me! I had started to feel sick, with my stomach churning round - all signs that I was starting to recognise when He was challenging me on something that was important and often difficult. I also knew what it was linked with! Do you remember me sharing, back in Ch 2/2, about the Lord speaking to me about going on missionary work to India? Well, the thoughts about it had recently started coming back, and I had been asking the Lord about it - I realised that He was speaking to me about getting out of the boat and to start walking towards what He was showing me to do. So I went forward and Bryn prayed for me. That last visit to the Ipswich Convention turned out to be a very eventful one! You will be able to see, further on in my story, where and how the Lord took me overseas....

Something else I had begun to learn during my time in Daventry, was to recognise that God has a plan for every part of our lives and how it is so important to follow the leading of the Holy Spirit in order for us to be in the place He wants us to be, at the time He wants us to be! We used to emphasise the truth of this by saying to each other "See you in the Plan". The time when

I was in Ipswich when Bryn Jones spoke about Peter getting out of the boat - was very much an example of the importance of this. If I hadn't gone that year in response to the 'nudge' of the Spirit - I wouldn't have been there for Him to speak to me through Bryn.

I want to encourage you to ask the Lord to improve your ability to listen to the Spirit's leading. To ask Him to help you to be in the right place at the right time to hear what He wants to say to you! When you plan to meet up with friends even - learn to be sensitive in regard to what Father is wanting, so your time and fellowship is part of His plan for you, and will be productive as you share Jesus together.

Kingston Christian Fellowship

Another contact given to me quite early on through South Chard, was that of Timmy and Sheila Bateson, a couple who lived in Teddington, South London and not far from Kingston-upon-Thames. At that time in 1971, they also had a fellowship meeting in their home as a result of visiting the church at South Chard. My ears had pricked up when I first heard of that group, because of my friends Wendy and Doreen who lived in Streatham, who were looking for fellowship to grow deeper in the move of the Spirit. I remember visiting the fellowship around that time, when it was still meeting in the Bateson's home.

As the fellowship grew, it became too big to continue meeting in their home and it moved to Kingston Market Hall, and became Kingston Christian Fellowship. I visited a few times when it was there and began to get to know others in the fellowship, besides my friends Wendy and Doreen. Yes, they started going and, in fact, actually moved to that area from Streatham. By the time they moved there KCF was meeting in a church hall in Surbiton (although it continued to be called 'Kingston' Christian Fellowship) - and they moved into a flat in Surbiton rather than Kingston.

These links I began to make with KCF were all part of His plan. Amazingly, it wasn't a great length of time before I was also living in Surbiton and a part of KCF - and so were Peter and Jean and family! I will share how this came about in due course....

I don't believe that there are ever any coincidences with the Lord - even though they might look as though that's what they are to us! In fact, in Jeremiah, God's Word says that He set us apart even before we were born - that means He has His plans for us all sorted right from before we enter this world. Think what that means in your life! Nothing that happens to you takes your Father by surprise. - and He already has the answer and response planned. I mean, how amazing is that?

'413' - Ipswich Fellowship

Back in the early part of Ch 4 I shared about my first visit to the Ipswich Convention and, quite soon after that, the Whitson weekend of ministry at Woodbridge School not far away from Ipswich town. And that was the very beginning of the links forged with Freda, her family and those who were part of the fellowship at '413'..... As well as staying with Muriel for one of the Easter conventions, I also stayed with her and the family one summer, during my time teaching in Daventry, and had the opportunity to go to the meetings at 413. Muriel, and another friend, also visited me in my flat in Daventry.

It was while I was living in Daventry that I first met and started to get to know Freda - but it was several years later when I saw more of her and we got to know each other properly! And, yes, I will share more about that later in my story....

I look back now at those four years ('71 through to '74) and only now do I fully realise the preparation the Lord laid down in my life for the future. I'm not sure if the word 'preparation' is the most appropriate word to use, but I think it's the one that best sums up what He did during that time. He brought me into contact with so many of His Family that went on to play quite a pivotal role in my life - some right through the years to come; some just for one or two seasons.

I think of Ananias, in Acts, being sent to pray for Paul to receive back his sight and how that, in fact, is the only time we hear of him - but look at how important that one act of obedience turned out to be. Be obedient to the leading of the Spirit in regard to meeting people and doing and sharing what He shows you.... It might be a one off occasion, one of several meetings or the start of something lasting for much longer - but, whichever it is, remember that the Lord has a purpose and a desire to accomplish something that is part of His plan, even though He might not ever share with you what that may be.

CHAPTER 5

Lessons in Obedience to God

5/1 Back in London – Preparation Time

Time to get out of the boat!

After the Lord spoke to me at the Easter Convention in 1974 about 'getting out of the boat, I arrived home in Daventry knowing that I had to do something about it. I believe the Lord had been stirring things up in my spirit, prior to that word about the boat, and reminding me of how He'd spoken to me about going to India.

So often the Lord only takes us one step at time when He's showing us what's on His heart for us - and this time was no exception. With my previous connection with BMMF (Bible and Medical Missionary Fellowship) through helping at the children's camps, and helping in their main office occasionally between my college terms - it seemed to be the best place to start. Added to which it was where my friends Wendy and Doreen, now living in Surbiton, also worked.

I made contact with the BMMF office in London and arranged a meeting with Arthur Pont, who was the person leading the fellowship at that time. By the way, all this would have begun to get underway after coming back from Ipswich, and back at school after the Easter school holidays. So, this took place during the summer term, as I would need to give my notice into school to finish at the end of term - towards the end of July, when school started the summer break. I think I must have arranged to go down to London to discuss things at BMMF during the half term, at the end of May - the week of the bank holiday.

After talking it all through with Arthur, someone I'd always got on well with, I found that quite understandably, he had reservations about sending me out on the mission field (the terminology used back then!). He knew of my attempted suicide, as my friend Wendy had been his PA at the time; and he knew me as well from when I'd helped with the summer camps, and worked in the office in between college terms. Apparently Wendy was with him when she got the news of what had happened, was upset and had shared it with him. And Doreen was running the General Office there at that time also and by then, I knew a fair number of the people working there!

He was concerned about BMMF's responsibility for me working in India - which was the proposed country we were talking about my going to. But he was also concerned for me, and how well I would cope with the difficulties that I would face with working there. Would I be emotionally and mentally capable in that sort of situation in view of the breakdown that had happened previously? I was initially concerned about the result of my first conversation with him about it - partly, I think, because I had it so firmly in my own spirit that this was what the Lord had showed me. But, I also quite understood his reservations and why!

However, the result of that meeting wasn't a categorical 'no' - my Father was at work again! After thinking about it, and presumably discussing it with others within BMMF, they came up with a suggestion.... This suggestion was that I should actually go and work at the BMMF office for a year - basically in order that I could be assessed on how I coped generally and, especially, what I was like when I was under pressure.

This, in fact, was my next step on the current path that the Lord was leading me on at that time. The first step was the word He'd given me about 'getting out of the boat', that came through Bryn. But, if I hadn't moved out on that, He wouldn't have been able to show me the next step. Remember, if you're asking the Lord to show you where to go, or what to do next - you need to be moving.... He'll show you something but, unless you trust Him and move out in faith on it - He won't be able to show you what to do next. He called Abraham out of Ur - but He didn't tell him, until he'd left Ur behind, where He was going to take him. The wonderful thing is that, if we start moving and it's the wrong direction, because we are on the move Father can step in and help change the direction so we're moving to where He wants us to be!

Back in London and Working at BMMF

The suggestion that I work at the BMMF office was, I felt, my next step and was at peace that this was what the Lord wanted me to do. Changes were already happening in the office at Kennington, as Wendy was leaving, believing the Lord wanted her to move on. Doreen also had a move - but hers was within the office, as she took over as Arthur's PA after Wendy left. It was planned for me to work in the General Office, the main reception area, with a view to taking on the running of the office in due course. There was another, older lady, also working there called Maureen. She, and her flat mate Jean, were also part of KCF (Kingston Christian Fellowship), as Wendy and Doreen were - and I knew them from when I'd visited KCF.

The Lord was very gracious when He moved me back to work in London - He took me to a place that I was already familiar with, several people there I also already knew and with a basic knowledge of the work being covered. How great was that!?

Somewhere to Live

It was quite hard to pack up my flat and move to London, looking at it from a 'natural' point of view. But having such a certainty in my heart that this was the next step that Father had planned for me, made all the difference. I realise even more now that when the tide turns, it doesn't just stop. It keeps flowing on, and this time it was flowing in the direction that would prepare me for going overseas. Yes, I had no doubt that, after a year proving the stability that the Lord had given me when He turned the tide - that I'd be off!

But I did need somewhere to live in the meantime..... Initially my dear friends Wendy and Doreen, once again let me stay with them. Only this time the circumstances couldn't have been more different. I should also explain that Christine, Peter and Jean's eldest daughter had also moved down to Kingston, by the time I got there - staying with a friend. We planned to look for somewhere to share together, although it was no easier to find accommodation in London then, than it is now..... My vehicle at that time was an old style Bedford CF250, which I'd had for some time while still living in Daventry. This definitely made things easier from the point of view of having our own transport to get to work from wherever we ended up living!

There was a girl called Janet, also working at BMMF, who lived in Leytonstone and had her own house. She invited Chris and myself to live with her whilst we continued to look for somewhere more suitable in the Kingston / Surbiton area, where we were becoming part of KCF and went on a regular basis. Again, both of us knew folk in the fellowship and felt that was where we should be based church wise. I was very grateful to Wendy and Doreen helping me - but Chris needed to move on from where she was staying, and by then we were flat hunting in earnest.

Eventually a flat came up in Surbiton, in the road that ran parallel to the main high street and opposite a supermarket. You entered the supermarket on foot from the main street, but drove into the car park from an entrance just by the flat. To say it was 'in a state' was an understatement! But it had a kitchen, one small and one very large bedroom, and a decent sized lounge. If we took it, it would mean decorating it completely - after it had a good clean..... It was what you might call a challenge - but, because of the state it was in, it wasn't a high rent! We took it!

Have you found that sometimes the Lord answers your prayers in a completely unexpected way, and have found it to be a real challenge? For me, this was one of those occasions! There was so much work to be done, albeit mainly decorating, but with us both working full time - yes, it was a challenge..... But we both believed this was the flat the Lord had taken us to in answer to our prayers, although we didn't fully realise why, until much later. We got the small bedroom straight first, which would be for Chris - but also used it as our place to relax in between working on the rest of the rooms!

We eventually got the flat sorted out as to how we wanted it and then had more time to live our lives in a more normal way.... We got involved in the life of KCF and were able to get to know better those in the fellowship whom we had already had contact with prior to actually living in the area. Plus, of course, making a whole load of new friends as well.

Crunch Time!

With the approach of the summer of '75 we began to look at the way forward.... BMMF seemed satisfied with taking me on to work overseas after my time running what was generally known as the 'front' office. Unfortunately, at that particular time there didn't appear to be any vacancies in India; or anywhere else for that matter! Arthur Pont felt it might be helpful to liaise with

CMS (Church Missionary Society) with a view to sending me to one of their placements jointly with BMMF. We never found out whether it would have worked as, to cut a long story short - I ended up being considered for a CMS post in Isfahan, Iran, and going out with CMS.

It was arranged that I go on an 'assessment' weekend with CMS - where the assessors would meet and talk with me, and then make a decision. I thought that probably the main thing that might stop me being accepted, would be my history of the suicide attempt..... I wasn't accepted to go forward, but the reason was completely different. The panel of assessors felt that they didn't think I would fit in with what they called the 'Anglican setup' in Isfahan. The reason for this conclusion was my involvement in the house church fellowships I'd been with over the previous 4 to 5 years.

I had a letter from the panel after the weekend to explain their decision and why they had made it. After that, I really didn't have a clue as to what to do next and realised I needed to leave it in the Lord's hands and let Him show me. Praise the Lord - He didn't keep me in suspense for very long! It was only a few days before I had another letter from the panel - asking me if I'd be willing to meet up with Bishop Hassan Dehqani-Tafti, the Anglican Bishop in Iran, when he visited England in a few days time. I didn't delay in letting them know that, yes, I was happy to meet him.

I found out later what had happened. CMS had already discussed with Bishop Hassan, the possibility of my going out to Isfahan. The morning after it had been decided that I wasn't suitable - they received a letter from the Bishop saying how pleased he was that I would be going to join them. At that point the decision was made to arrange for us to meet - and let the Bishop decide whether he would be happy to have me working with him in Isfahan at the girl's hostel, which was where I would be based. We met up, as arranged and the rest, as is often said, was history! The Bishop decided he wanted me to go - and things started moving.....

Sometimes a door, which we think is already beginning to open - suddenly closes! That's what happened with the 'door' I had begun to go through with CMS on my way, I thought, to going out to work in Iran. Sometimes we have to be willing to do nothing, but leave it all in God's hands for Him to sort out. More often than not, it is difficult not to step in and try and work it out for ourselves. In this instance Father was very gracious to me - I didn't have a clue as to how I might work it out, or what to do otherwise! But God had already got it all planned out.

Never be afraid to trust the Lord to sort out a situation that might have arisen that you have no idea how to salvage, and seems impossible. If He tells you to do something - do it. If He doesn't - don't! It's so important to listen and be obedient at these times. God will do what we can't - but we do need to listen carefully as to whether there is anything He's asking of us.

Preparation Time for Iran

It turned out that I was needed in Iran in the January of 1976 in order to start my training to take over from Christine, who was currently running the hostel; and to also start language lessons in Farsi, the Persian language. Actually this was good timing, as it had been August when the decision was finally made that I would be going. This meant that I could go to the CMS Training College in Sellyoak, Birmingham for the autumn term, prior to heading for Isfahan in the January.

I hadn't in fact, had a great deal of contact with CMS prior to all this happening - so it was helpful to have the time at Sellyoak before I left for Iran. As well as learning more about CMS and it's structure etc, we were introduced and instructed in some of the basic things we needed to know about being on the mission field. Also, of course, we looked at the ethics of working on the mission field. Plus those biblical principles it entailed, etc.

We also learned about how we would be linked with various parishes who were interested in the country we were going to and wanting to partner with us in prayer back up, etc. Where possible we were asked to make contact and try and visit these parishes before we left. Then, once we were overseas, we were requested to keep in touch and let them know how things were progressing.

Why was the Flat so Important?

Earlier, I shared that both Chris and myself really felt the flat in Surbiton was the one the Lord led us to - in spite of the state it was in. We got it sorted out and we enjoyed living there and it was also in a very convenient position in Surbiton. Then, around the time I was preparing to go to Sellyoak, we heard the news that Peter and Jean and Chris' three sisters - Janie, Karen and Joanna were coming down to live in London!

It was at that point, I think, we began to realise why the Lord had given us that particular flat! The lay out of the flat was able to easily accommodate the whole family - including me. Peter and Jean were able to have the small bedroom, and the large bedroom was easily large enough for the four girls - and me as well, when I needed to be there. Long term it wouldn't necessarily have worked, but initially it was fine, as the Lord showed them the next step of their journey in their new season. It coincided with me going off to Sellyoak - so I wasn't going to be around that much.....

Yet again the Lord's timing and planning was just so 'on the ball'! No wonder we were given such certainty about taking that flat - the Lord knew it wasn't just for us, but for the whole family. At that point we had no idea that He was going to move the rest of the family down from Daventry, and had already had it planned. And the timing, with me going off to Sellyoak.... Chris had the rest of the family with her and wouldn't be in that big flat on her own. Father is always so thoughtful and loving in the way He works it all out.

It was another lesson in realising how important it is to listen and be led by the Holy Spirit - in every single part of your life. Don't disregard His 'nudges' but go with what He tells you. Remember, it's not just important in what Father wants to do in your life - it's also important for those you're in fellowship with in His family as well as, very often, your natural family. Don't find you're suddenly living with regret, because you didn't act on His leading

5/2 Iran and New Lessons to Learn

Flying into a New Season

It was 6th January 1976, I believe, when I flew out of Heathrow and headed for Tehran, the capital city of Iran - the first time I had flown anywhere on my own! We stopped off at Moscow on the way - my memory mainly being the blast of very cold air coming into the plane when the door was opened, and I was so glad that we didn't need to go out into it! We arrived in Tehran in the evening, which meant I couldn't travel on to Isfahan, my destination, until the next day. A kind couple met me, arranged by CMS, and I stayed with them before continuing my journey to Isfahan. Again I was met on arrival and taken to the Girls' Hostel - which I thought would be my home in Isfahan for the next three years, before going home on furlough. Once more I was going to find out that my Father had other plans - but once again I'm getting ahead of myself, and I will share that in due course!

It's easy to think of Iran as being a hot country, and it is - but not in the middle of winter, which is when I arrived..... In fact it gets very cold, as I would learn in my three years living there, with heavy falls of snow. However, there was a redeeming feature - it was a 'dry' cold (not 'damp' like the UK) and, best of all it was mostly bright and sunny, even if the sun didn't hold any warmth, and the sky was nearly always a wonderful blue colour!

Life at the Hostel in Isfahan

The Iranian girls who lived in the hostel were mainly there in order to attend school in Isfahan - due to living in out lying villages that didn't have the education provision needed for the older aged children. Another CMS missionary, Chris was running the hostel and the aim of my arrival on the scene was to learn the 'ropes' from her in order to eventually take over; and release her to move on. We got on well together.

One of my main tasks initially was to get stuck into learning Farsi, the language spoken in Iran - not Arabic which is spoken mostly in the Middle East. I had a lovely lady who came regularly to teach me. She was the 'second' wife of the man who was her husband - my first contact with the Islamic situation where a man can have 4 wives and as many temporary ones as he wants!

We each had a 'day off' every week and, in order to have a proper break, would go and stay on the mission compound with some of the nursing staff who worked at the hospital, which was based there. Betty, one of the senior missionaries, would come up to the hostel to help me when Chris had her day off. I needed that help in the early days as I was learning what was entailed in running the hostel - and, of course, with very little language at my command initially, it would have been a complete shambles without her.

In some respects my time working for a year in the children's home had helped and prepared me for living and working in the hostel. But I don't think it's possible to be fully prepared for living in another country full time, when you don't know the culture and haven't a clue what people are saying to you - or possibly about you. It's something that takes time to adjust to!

I began to learn the routine of the hostel, as well as of the country. Thursday and Friday became the 'weekend', because Friday was the day the people went to the local mosque - in the same way as Christians go to church on Sunday. The Jewish people had Friday and Saturday, as their Sabbath day was Saturday, and the Christians Saturday and Sunday. However, the 'official weekend' in the country, was Thursday and Friday, due to it being an Islamic based country. As a result - the girls attended school from Saturday through to Wednesday, and enjoyed their weekend at home on Thursday and Friday! I have fond memories of relaxing in the TV room and having toasted sandwiches for a treat - rather than sitting up at the dining table for a more formal meal!

On Sunday evenings Chris and I would head for the evening service being held at the Episcopalian Church in Isfahan (the equivalent of the Anglican Church in the UK). There were occasions when we would go one route and return on another - just as a precaution, if we'd heard about any trouble in the city! Some of the girls who wanted to, would come with us - curious, I believe, to find out more about what many thought of as a 'Western' religion.

As I look back at those first few months at the hostel in Isfahan, I am so grateful for the way the Lord looked after me. Grateful for the way Chris and I got on so well together - we had never met previously to my arrival on the doorstep, and, because of the nature of the work we were involved in, we spent most of

our time together. Grateful to Chris for her patience with me as I began to learn the multitude of things I needed to know - not only within the hostel, but in Isfahan as well; not to mention the country as a whole! Grateful for the way the Lord helped me to get a grasp of the things I needed to know as priority - and then continued to teach me throughout my time in the country.

I want to encourage you not to be daunted by the task(s) the Lord sets before you and calls you to do! I believe that He wouldn't call you if He hadn't already got it all planned out; and He definitely wouldn't call you unless He was going to help you and equip you to carry it out. He says in His Word: "Faithful is he that calleth you, who also will do it." 1 Thessalonians 5:24 KJV. If you stand on His promise in His Word, and are obedient to the call He has given you - you can move forward step by step into all He has planned for you. But don't expect your feelings to come into line straight away with it all - so often we have to start moving, still feeling a bit 'wobbly' about it all! But, and this is the amazing thing, as you move forward - you'll suddenly realise you're no longer wobbly, but have a certainty in your spirit concerning what your Father is asking you to do.

Challenges to be Faced

My first two or three months were challenging as I've already shared - from the point of everything being new, including the language! Then there came another challenge, that I wasn't expecting - a challenge to my health....

In fact, I ended up with several challenges to my health during my time in Isfahan; with a bad bout of shingles early summer, followed by an attack of para-typhoid towards the autumn in that first year. I'd had all my vaccinations before going out there and was so thankful that it wasn't full blown typhoid! I was also very thankful to the Lord for our CMS doctors at the mission hospital in Isfahan. As part of my recovery I was sent down to the lovely city of Shiraz, down in the south of the country. I spent a week staying with two missionaries whilst there and it was a precious week of fellowship that Father graciously gave us.

So I spent a good part of that first year trusting the Lord through the attacks on my health! And was very grateful to those at home who were supporting me in prayer. I had no doubt that I was where the Lord had put me, and that gave me such strength not to let the enemy be successful.

I have found that sometimes we have to be determined and persevere through a situation, stand on God's Word and tell the enemy where to go! One of the Words He gave me before I set off for Iran was Joshua's famous encouragement that he received from the Lord when he was told he would be leading the Israelites after Moses was no longer there. "...Be strong and very courageous....Be not afraid....for the Lord your God is with you wherever you go..." (Joshua 1:9). What more could I ask for, but to know my Father was with me? And I know that covered where I was, and included everything I was doing!

Remember, when you pray for people working in other countries, that they aren't necessarily exempt from attacks on their health - if anything they are often more vulnerable and become targets of the enemy!

Iranian Hospitality

The people of Iran have a tremendous reputation in regard to their hospitality. They love gathering together in their family groups, including the extended family, and spending time together - and especially if they can combine it with a picnic out in the park and spend the whole day together! They are no less hospitable to those from elsewhere living amongst them. Chris and I were often invited to the homes of people in Isfahan that we met, and it was lovely to be made so welcome.

We also went on a much longer visit in the summer of '77, after school had broken up in early June when it starts to get really hot! One of the girls at the hostel came from the Qashqai tribe - one of the many nomadic tribes in Iran, who speak a dialect called Torki as their main language, but also speak Farsi the Persian language used in the country. In the summer months they lived in the highland pastures north of Shiraz, but took their flocks 300 miles south to winter pastures on lower lands, which were warmer, near the Persian Gulf. Chris and I were invited to visit her family in their tribal village up on the highland pastures - where it was much cooler in the hot months.

The week we spent there really was a wonderful experience and insight into such a completely different world. Everyone made us so welcome and we met an awful lot of people through the week. On the day we arrived one of our first sights was of a man skinning a goat very skilfully - and learned that we were having goat as part of our first evening meal. It was also explained that the skin was taken off very carefully because it would later be used to carry water from the stream.

And that was just the beginning of our time there! We were also later shown how they spun the wool from the sheep, and then how the weaving was done - all of it by hand, no machines. It was a privilege to have been invited and included in their tribal way of life for the week we were there.

Change is Afoot

Towards the end of the school year, probably May of '77, I had no sense that the coming months were going to bring quite drastic changes into my life. I did realise that the time was probably on the horizon for Chris to move on - and that I would be responsible for the hostel. But, other than that, I had no idea....

So often I've found that it was better for me not to know everything from the beginning - because I'm not sure that I would have been able to go through with it.... But God is always so patient and understanding and knows just how much we can cope with; and His timing is always perfect.

To explain as simply as I can.... There was a teaching vacancy in the Henry Martyn School in Tehran - an American International Christian School. The age group was Kindergarten up to Grade 6, the equivalent of our top Juniors in the UK; and taught, obviously, in the American Grade system which was somewhat different to our system. Chris went through the necessary processes - and was offered a teaching post there. However, there were in fact two vacancies and therefore they actually needed two teachers at the school.....

Well..... that so caught my attention, and I couldn't stop

thinking about that second teaching post in Tehran. But, at the same time it seemed ridiculous, as I had been invited by the Bishop to take over the care of the hostel in Isfahan from Chris - and that's what I'd been getting prepared for….

Have you ever experienced that? You get a thought, which seems absolutely ridiculous, but it keeps niggling at you and just will not go away. Then you think maybe it is the Lord, but how on earth do you tell anyone about it - especially those in authority over you; which in my case was Bishop and CMS.

Eventually I realised that, ignoring it wasn't the answer - because it just would not go away. I had to do something in response to what I was thinking and feeling - I was no longer at peace in my spirit, and when that happens I know the Lord is speaking to me…. I knew that I needed to take some sort of a step forward towards what I'd begun to think He wanted me to do - and trust Him to lead me and show me the way.

I had the necessary conversations with the school, the Bishop and with CMS. My meeting with Bishop was difficult and, understandably, he was upset and couldn't really understand me wanting to leave the hostel to go and teach in Tehran. On the surface it appeared that I'd broken my commitment, and the only reason I could give was that I believed it was what God wanted and that I had to be obedient. Bishop was a 'man of God' but he found it difficult to understand how I could be so certain that it was God - and not just something that I wanted and preferred to do!

The response I received at first from CMS was that I was under the authority of the Bishop and I should do what he was saying I should do - remain in Isfahan at the hostel. But it was eventually agreed in principle that I could go to Tehran and, as I was going to be back in England in July, we could talk it through in more detail whilst I was there. Yes, I was going back for a month, and God's timing couldn't have been more perfect!

An Unexpected, but Timely Gift

As if our unexpected trip to visit the Qashqai tribal people wasn't enough of a bonus that summer - I was given a special gift from the Lord.... They had a 'Love Offering' for me in my home church, KCF, which paid for a return ticket from Isfahan to London. For those who've not come across this before... the morning offering on a particular Sunday was to be given to me. In the fellowship which I was part of we used to call it a 'Love Offering'- because that was what it was, an offering of money given out of love to me. A very humbling gift, and it meant a great deal to me.

Chris decided to have a trip home as well and it was great that we were able to travel back together and we were able to have the necessary conversations with CMS about the way forward. And, of course, it was great to visit our family and friends.

I didn't fully realise, until later, how gracious the Lord had been in providing for me to go back home for that month. Not all that long after I had returned to Iran, I received a letter from my parents which contained rather challenging news. I need to explain that, back at the end of the '60's, during the three years I was training for teaching - my mother was rushed into hospital, where they discovered ovarian cysts which the medics removed. I obviously knew all about that - but the letter that came after I was back in Isfahan, was to say that my mother had now been diagnosed as suffering from ovarian cancer.

My parents hadn't told me before I left because they knew it would have been very difficult for me to return if I knew the situation. Her ovaries would be removed and then she would need to have radio-therapy treatment. My mother suffered badly from emphysema - any operation would be risky from the point of view of the anaesthetic. As you can imagine it was a shock but also a challenge! I was too far away to help in any practical way - but I could definitely pray, and I could ask others to pray as well.

When I wrote back to my parents in response to their letter, I told them that I was praying that the Lord would bring my mother through the operation - and through the strain of having to travel a distance every week day for five weeks in order to have the radio-therapy treatment. And then I went on to explain that I was also in the process of writing to all my friends to ask them to pray as well!

As you can well imagine, that was a testing time but, by God's grace, He brought me through. But, more than that, He also brought my mother through. Yes, wonderfully, she lived for another five years after that. Just before her death, she actually saw the consultant who had operated on her 5yrs previously - apparently he couldn't believe that she had lived another five years! During those years I saw the Lord's hand upon her life. Even to the point of having a neighbour who was in the Salvation Army and loved the Lord who, every time Mum had to go for her check up, she reminded her not to forget that her daughter and her friends were praying for her....

I trust this is an encouragement to those of you facing difficult and challenging situations at this time. Don't give up! Ask the the Lord what you should do - 'wait', if He tells you to, or 'act' if that's what He leads you to do. In the situation with my mother I 'knew' I had to pray - not just because it was my mother, but because that's what the Lord laid on my heart to do. And, as I shared earlier, to contact all my friends and ask them to pray as well. I can't stress how important it is to ask the Lord, and not just do what you think you should. Remember, it's no surprise to Him - He's already planned the answer to give to you.....

5/3 Tehran and a Revolution to get Through

Getting Settled in Tehran

On our return from the UK, we had a busy time moving from Isfahan and settling into the flat we found in Tehran. The Lord was very gracious to us and we moved into a first floor flat, owned by a lovely Iranian couple who lived on the ground floor. We all got on very well together and they played quite a part in helping us to settle in. We sorted out how to get to the school via the bus, until we were able to get a car, which made life a great deal easier! I think we both enjoyed teaching at the school. Later in the school year, during the summer term I believe, the Headteacher felt it was time for her to move on, and Chris was asked if she would consider taking over - which she accepted.

Outside of the school we became part of the Episcopalian church in Tehran, so we were still in contact with Bishop and his family. We also got to know quite a number of expatriates, many of whom were American. That first Christmas we were invited back to Isfahan, to spend it with Bishop and his family. We were driving down, but had to make sure that we had snow chains to use on our car in case they were needed. All vehicles leaving Tehran at that time of the year had to either have snow tyres or snow chains with them.... and were checked! We had a lovely Christmas in Isfahan, and it was good to see all our friends there.

As I've been sharing this with you, I've been struck by the humility of Bishop in inviting me into his home - after the

disruption I would have caused him in leaving to go and teach in Tehran, instead of staying at the hostel in Isfahan. Going back to visit, I don't remember sensing any sign of 'aggro' in our time together that Christmas, and felt completely at peace. I don't know about you - but that was definitely a lesson learned for me....

Another Trip to England

Chris and I took another trip home in the July of '78, and it was good to be in the 'normality' of home for a while - things were very restless politically in Iran, and especially in Tehran. The Lord blessed me with another gift from the fellowship, which was so kind of them. Once again it was lovely to see friends and family and catch up with everyone, and especially good to see how my mother was continuing to progress.

I also spent some time staying with Peter and Jean and, before I returned to Iran, we went up together to visit Barbara and her family in Northampton, where they had moved to from Daventry. It was during that weekend, as we were praying together, that one of them had a word from the Lord for me, saying that He was taking me back to Iran for a season. I didn't really understand fully what He meant - but knew it was important and that I needed to hold on to it.....

If you're given a word, and you know in your spirit it really is from the Lord, it's important to hold onto it - whether you understand it or not. That's when you have to trust and believe that Father will show you what He's saying to you - at the time you need to know! This was one of those occasions.... and I will

share with you later, why that word was so important to me, when the Lord gave me understanding of the meaning of it.

Living Through a Revolution!

Various demonstrations began to take place off and on through '78, and in the autumn they became more widespread, numerous, larger and more fierce in nature. As we started the Autumn term we realised that there would be challenges ahead..... Demonstrations on 8th September 1978 were particularly widespread and violent as nearly 90 people died, resulting in it being called Black Friday - and at midnight martial law in Tehran and another 11 major cities was declared.

In September through to November street demonstrations continued and this was very much the case in Tehran. My classroom had a window looking out onto the street and, from where my desk was situated, I had a clear view. I remember on one afternoon looking out and seeing armed soldiers running up the road. I knew if the children got any hint of them being there, they would have rushed to the window to see them! I managed to keep their attention on what I was doing with them, and it was a great relief when I registered the fact that the soldiers had passed by.

There were many disruptions to normal life during this time due to nationwide strikes and a general strike was declared in October. The disrupted electrical supplies particularly affected the lives of most people. So much so we had to kit ourselves out with supplies of candles for use when the electricity went off - usually around 9pm in the evening.

On 5th November demonstrations, originating in the University of Tehran and spreading over the whole of the city, became violent and destructive. Many buildings and vehicles were set on fire and even piles of tyres. We got information sent to us in school of some of what was happening, and got all the students home as early as was possible in the afternoon. I remember standing on the roof of our flat and looking over the city and all we could see were burning fires. My most memorable 'bonfire night' ever! It was after this that we felt we had to close the school because of the safety of the students whilst there, as well as the travelling to and fro.

I've endeavoured to give you an insight into some of the occurrences through this time and some idea of the challenges we faced. There is a great deal more that happened, but that isn't really in my remit to detail at length. What I want to share above all is the many, many ways we experienced God's love and care through those months. We were so aware of Him alerting us to particular dangers, and how He kept us safe when we had to travel about in the city. Remember, we were westerners and weren't very popular, although it was the Americans in particular that were really disliked.

You can always be sure that if the Lord allows you to be in difficult and dangerous situations - His angels are there taking caring of you. It was in the early days of the revolution that the Lord reminded me of the word He gave me when my friends prayed - the fact that He was taking me back to Iran for a season..... It gave me such stability because I knew He would see me through all that was happening - and take me safely back to

the UK afterwards. Hallelujah!

Heading Back to the UK

As the year ended and we entered a new one, the revolution escalated - the Shah left and the Revolutionary guards were everywhere. There were food shortages, fuel needing to be queued for and the power supplies were even more erratic, in that we never knew when everything would go dark - at least before it was at 9 pm on a regular basis! Chris had returned from a couple of weeks at home over Christmas, and we began to think about packing up the flat - not knowing for how much longer we would be there....

By the time we were into January and my third year 'anniversary' in the country - all my papers (particularly my Work Visa) allowing me to be there, ran out! This meant I was there illegally and couldn't leave until they were renewed, at that stage that wasn't going to happen, as all the relevant offices had closed....

We were advised to pack as much as possible into a case and make a move to the Diocesan Centre in the middle of Tehran - and book a flight out. We were given to understand that as long as the offices were closed we would be allowed out without the necessary, up to date paperwork. We also packed a trunk each with the thought that we might be able to get it sent back to the UK at some time in the future (and this did actually happen!).

Well, we made the move, and booked the flight - and then the airport was closed! This was after there was a lot of activity from the Revolutionary guards on the roads round about, which pretty well encircled the Centre. We found out as things progressed, that the TV station was in the process of being taken over.... At some stage during this time we were given a tip off that the banks might be closing. We were so thankful to the Lord for alerting us to this as went there straight away and, amazingly, were the last ones able to withdraw our cash. There were many others in the queue behind us who were unable to.

Then we heard from the British Embassy that the RAF were in negotiations with the authorities to enable them to fly into Tehran airport, to pick up the many British expatriates in the country. We found when we did arrive home that there had been a great deal about it on the news in UK - and everyone knew far more than us about it!

Again, I wanted to give you some idea of our experiences in those last days in Tehran. It's history now that the RAF came in and took one plane out - and then all the necessary offices opened, and after that your paperwork had to be renewed before you could depart..... I do praise the Lord that Chris and I were on that first flight out. Hallelujah! Those who weren't took quite some time before they were able to leave because of renewing their paperwork. Mind you, our exit also included a rather scary ride up to the embassy, where we would be then taken to the airport - we were stopped half a dozen times by guards who very noticeably had shotguns at the ready. And also some one was shot in the airport while we were there.

This again was a time for really leaning on the Lord and listening to what He was saying we should do. He's always one

step ahead with events which, as He's in charge of the planning, He would be! We moved around the city as and when we felt it was safe to and we were at peace in the Lord. I've shared already how we were able to draw out our money from the bank when we went - the last ones to do so at that point. And then He made sure we were on the first RAF flight out as He would know that the offices would open later that day..... What a mighty God we serve!

Arriving Home!

We flew from Tehran to Nicosia in Cyprus with the RAF and were then transferred on to a commercial flight to fly to Heathrow. We actually were given the option of staying over in Nicosia if we wanted to, and this is what Chris and Ian (by then Chris' fiancé) chose to do. I continued to Heathrow and Peter and Jean came and picked me up late on the Saturday night. I stayed with them the Saturday and Sunday nights, which was great as I was able to go to KCF and thank everyone for their support and prayer. Then on the Monday, they drove me down to Folkestone to my parents' home.

On the way home from the airport Jean explained that she was so sure I'd be home on that first flight - she'd prepared a bed and got extra food out of the freezer for 'Sunday lunch'! I think my first impression of being home was that everything seemed so sensible and calm - in comparison to where I'd come from.....

It thrilled me that the Lord had prepared Peter and Jean for my arrival home and had spoken so clearly to them. And I was so blessed at the timing of it all, that enabled me to visit the

fellowship prior to going back to my parents' home in Folkestone. If I hadn't gone then I wasn't sure when it would have been possible....

Tying Up the Ends

Those of us returning home from Iran had some 'time out' at home with our families to recover from the time we'd been through, prior to leaving Iran. It did seem a bit strange at first to no longer be in the intensity of atmosphere that we'd been in during the days of the revolution. But after a break, I went back up to London for 'de-briefing' with CMS and to talk about the way forward. I'd had nothing from the Lord about going anywhere else overseas - especially as He'd said very specifically that I was only going back for a season. It was agreed I'd continue with CMS for another 6 month and finish at the end of August. This gave me time to visit the various parishes that had supported me during my time out in Iran.

Whilst I was at CMS headquarters I was taken to one side by the 'chief' for a quiet word. It was very humbling actually, because he said, with hindsight, he understood exactly why the Lord had taken me to Tehran with Chris. You see, by the time of the revolution she had become the headteacher at the school and, in those very difficult days, needed all the support she could have. In her position she'd had to go to 'education' meetings with the authorities and make all sorts of decisions - not normally in the job description but necessary in the circumstances. Bless him, he thanked me for standing firm and being obedient to what the Lord had said to me..... so encouraging.

Only the Lord knew why I should go to Tehran and to the Henry Martyn school to teach alongside Chris, because He knew what was going to be happening. I thanked Him so much for helping me to stand firm and do what I believed He'd told me to, although I hadn't known why it was so important. I would encourage you to follow the leading of the Spirit - even when it doesn't make any sense to you, and others might disagree! I believe our Father loves it when we trust Him and do what He says, especially when we don't know why.....

CHAPTER 6

More Years of Training

6/1 Training Again in Surbiton

Lord - What's My Next Step?

Through my remaining time with CMS I enjoyed visiting the parishes I'd had support from - some of whom I'd met before going out to Iran, some I hadn't. I also went as a missionary 'rep' to a children's camp on the Norfolk Broads run by CMS. We camped on land and went out on the Broads on the boats during each day. I really enjoyed that.

Knowing my time with CMS was only until the end of August, I also needed to do something about work after that, plus of course finding somewhere to live! I believed that I was still part of the fellowship at KCF, especially after all the support they gave me whilst in Iran. Initially I was able to stay with my friends Peter and Jean, and then I moved into a shared flat in Surbiton with two or three other girls from KCF. I didn't feel I would be there for long and, in fact, another girl soon moved out of her flat to get married - and I was able to take it over!

It was a compact, two bed-roomed flat on the top floor of an old house, with a good sized lounge, a very small kitchen and a reasonably sized bathroom. One bed room was a good size, with space for two beds in fact - the other, little more than a box room, although it made me a very good office at a later date.... but that's rushing ahead a bit! I've given a fairly full description of the flat, because I actually ended up living there for 11 years.....

Work? Well, the obvious was to look for a teaching post, and I was at peace in doing that - so that's what I did! The local comprehensive in Surbiton, Hollyfield School, were advertising for an RE teacher, a full-time position - I applied, and was given the post. The bonus being that it was very near where I lived.

I very much felt that the Lord had showered me with His favour in giving me a flat, and a teaching post nearby. On top of that the hall where the fellowship met, was also nearby - and so was the flat where Peter and Jean lived. They lived on the site of the accommodation for, what was then the polytechnic, now Kingston University - who Peter worked for. I felt very blessed!

There are times when we seek the Lord's guidance, that He takes us along the path of doing something that's pretty obvious and the most sensible and natural for us to do. That's when it's easy, in many ways, to miss what He's saying. Why? It's because

we think that it needs to be complicated and challenging to our faith and hard to follow if it really is the Lord. And that's when we need to be really careful not to miss what He's saying to us, and assume it must be the enemy misleading us! We have such a gracious and loving Father. Hallelujah!

Starting Life in Surbiton

As I shared earlier, I was based in my flat for the next 11 years - years that I very much felt were another time of 'training' for me. I suppose, to a certain extent, when we are walking with the Lord we're in training until He takes us Home. But, I have found that there are seasons when I'm more aware of being taught / trained, and when often I feel the Lord is intent on taking me deeper in some of the areas He's taken me through before....

It would be great to say I settled easily back into life in England in my new home in the flat, and my new job in the school - but it wouldn't be honest of me to say so! It was good to be home, living near Peter and Jean and being able to become part of the fellowship. However, I did find that first term quite tough.... Looking back through the years from the present, I guess a good part of the reason was possibly reaction and recovering from living through the revolution in Iran.

But, I don't want to make that an excuse, as I think living on my own once again played a big part in it as well. At one point Peter actually asked whether I'd wanted to be up in Northampton and living near Barbara, but I said no - I think I'd begun to realise that I was letting my emotions get too much of a hold on me. I realised that the place I'd come to in Daventry and learning to live on my own - now needed to go deeper, and I asked the Lord to help me to do that.

As I shared with you, those first few months at my new school and at the flat were challenging! It was quite a relief when I began to realise and understand what the Lord was trying to teach me during that time. I find that sometimes, even though I might realise things aren't quite as they should be, I've not always been very quick off the mark to ask the Lord what's going on and what it is He's wanting me to learn from it. Sometimes I've asked the wrong questions - in as much as I've not really opened my heart up completely and been prepared to listen - whatever the answer might be! I do thank the Lord that sometimes, out of His love for me, He'll prompt someone close to me to ask a question, that will start me moving in the right direction.... like Peter did for me.

I would encourage you to have 'listening ears' in your spirit - and a listening heart as well! And that encouragement is for me also.... So often each one of us could save ourselves heartache, if we were more attentive to what Father wants to say to us - either directly or through someone else.

A Fairly Quiet Couple of Years!

My first couple of years working at Hollyfield School and living at my flat were fairly quiet, and reasonably uneventful, mostly! But it was also a time of learning and growing in the Lord and, to be honest, if you're walking forward and looking to the Holy Spirit to lead you - life will never be really quiet!

As I shared earlier - it was a time of going deeper into what it meant to be living on my own, and recognising I'll never actually live on my 'own', because Jesus is always with me! It was also a time of becoming more a part of KCF, from the point of actually being there - rather than at a distance of thousands of miles. Again, I've shared before about already knowing quite a few people there, and it was good to get to know a lot more of my brothers and sisters in the fellowship - especially the 'young mums' who were always glad of extra help with their children.

We had mid-week home groups - some on a Tuesday, some on a Wednesday. This was in order that various people could cover baby-sitting etc, in order that everybody who wanted to was able to attend one or other of the groups. It did work well.... It was also lovely to renew regular contact with Peter and Jean - and I often popped in for a cuppa after school. With Joanna being that much older by then, she was actually going to the school where I was teaching.....

It was during this time that I believe the Lord first spoke to me about writing a book - something I shared initially in Ch 3/2 under the heading "My Picture of the Sea". Such a shock! Even now, when I'm actually writing it, I sometimes pause and wonder if I've imagined it all. I think it's another 'gift' that Father gave to me when the 'tide turned'! It was a long time coming into being but, as I think I've said elsewhere - God is never in a hurry. I will share more about how it actually came about - at the appropriate time in my story.....

It possibly doesn't seem as though I was doing a great deal at that time that could be called 'training'! But, and I do realise

this the further I go on with Lord, He's training us every moment of every day - even, and maybe especially, when we don't realise it.... All the things we go through, large or small, good or bad, are opportunities to learn more. I appreciate the 'big' things He does in my life, but in many ways I appreciate even more the small things He does for me, that very often are only known to me alone!

Ripples of Change

It was early in '81 that I began to sense a sort of underlying ripple effect stirring in my spirit - not sure how else to describe it. I wasn't feeling 'down' in any way, or even discontented, yet I knew there was something resonating in my spirit - although I wasn't sure what. I had no idea what was happening - or why! But I did believe that, whatever was happening, was from the Lord and not the enemy - and trusted that, in due course, He'd show me.

Eventually, as I prayed about it, I began to feel that some sort of change was on the way. The majority of my lessons were RE, although I still did some games - as I had at Daventry. I still felt I should be teaching - but wasn't so sure it should be RE, as I became more and more aware of 'anti' feeling in the youngsters I taught. Not, I hasten to add, a reason for giving up teaching RE.... unless it was what the Lord was saying! I was beginning to wonder whether, if I was teaching a different subject, they would be more receptive to the things of the Lord. Actually, I found this was right..... but, again I am 'jumping the gun a bit!

I even wondered whether I should move to teaching the junior age group, as I had in Tehran, as they seemed so much more receptive to all subjects - including RE. I don't remember the 'ins and outs' of it but, early in the summer term, I became aware of a course to obtain a Diploma in the teaching of Business Studies. I'd made some enquiries by then about possibly getting a Degree of some sort - but it wasn't very straight forward as I had never studied for, or obtained, any A Levels. Then, I got the information about a year's re-training to teach Business Studies.

With my 'office' background, that also included proficiency in PAYE and pay rolls, etc - it seemed that maybe that was the way ahead. Especially with the upsurge of new technology, etc that was starting to happen back in '81! I made the necessary enquiries needed about the course itself. Then came the task of approaching the local Education Authority, to find out whether it was possible for them to send me on the course!

By then I knew in my heart that, if the Lord opened the door, I would go through it. But I also knew that, if it closed, then I'd move towards teaching in a junior school. My preference would be the top juniors - but remained open to whatever Father opened up for me.....

For many of us, change doesn't come easily - and I don't think I'm any different. It's so easy to become 'comfortable' in our familiar surroundings, with familiar people around us, and a familiar work pattern! But I have learned, and am still learning, how important it is for us to be open to any change that Father has on His heart for us. Sometimes it's an obvious change - which I believe is what happened when I returned from Iran. But, sometimes it's not obvious at all and we really have to listen carefully to what the Spirit is saying to us - and move forward a

step at a time as it's revealed to us. However, in both scenarios at the core is our willingness to be obedient. So really it's 'two-pronged', as we not only have to say to the Lord we'll be obedient - we also have to actually take some action. We can say 'yes' to being obedient - but, unless we take the action He reveals to us, it really doesn't mean a thing.

So, my question to you, as you read this today - "Is there anything that you're aware of, that Father has asked you to do and, although you said 'yes' - you haven't actually done anything?" Or - did you not even get to the point of saying 'yes' to His request? If you aren't aware of anything - may I suggest you just check, just in case He did ask you and you missed it! Far better to know, one way or the other....

6/2 New Adventures With the Lord

A New Adventure

I am guessing that having a year out to do nothing but study, isn't everyone's idea of an adventure! At one time I would have agreed... but, somehow I have a different outlook on it when I'm certain it's been arranged by the Lord. Don't forget either, that when He turned the tide in my life He then went on to 'turn' other things - and especially the way I looked at things. I knew, without a shadow of doubt, that when He saved me from the suicide attempt and later turned the tide of my life around - that the future was completely taken care of and He'd planned it all in love.

Once again, as things began to be made clear to me about being trained to teach Business Studies - I saw the hand of God working it all out. Normally, if you take a year off school the condition, by the Education Authority is that at the end, when you've got the qualification, you go back and teach at your school for at least a year or more. The condition that I was given was that I would be paid my full teacher's salary, but... I wouldn't be able to go back to Hollyfield at the end, and they didn't have to give me a post at any other school within the authority.

At first I thought I'd misunderstood - but I hadn't and I was free, when I finished training, to work anywhere I chose to. I think it was probably at that point that I began to think that Father had something else 'up His sleeve' for me! I'll share more about that, further along the road.....

Studying Again!

Well, you can probably imagine my year at Southlands College, Wimbledon, which was where the course was run; was pretty intensive. I hadn't done any studying since I finished my teacher training - and that had been 12 years before! I knew that to get through I would have to commit myself to that, and that alone - I went to KCF on Sunday, but did very little other than that apart from studying. Obviously, I visited my parents regularly down in Folkestone and made sure I saw close friends, such as Peter and Jean who were such a support to me through it; but it was quite hard in many respects....

But God is faithful, and when He sets you on a path of His choosing, He always gives the ability to do it. It's a different outcome - if we decide to do the choosing. I'm glad to say I passed all my examinations and left college with a Diploma in the Teaching of Business Studies, and qualified to teach the subject.

Back to Office Life

Towards the end of my year of study, when I needed to think about getting a job, I started asking the Lord what I should do next. We had a new family join the fellowship and I got to know Simon and Caroline quite well. He owned the Royal Kingston Laundry and they specialised in particular, in doing the laundry for many of the big hotels up in London, especially in the West End.

As I said, I became good friends with the family, who didn't live that far away from my flat. Around the time I was asking the

Lord what my next step would be, Simon began telling me of his need for a PA to work closely with him at the laundry. And that's where I ended up working for the next 18 months! Amazingly, if Simon wasn't around for any reason, he left me in charge.... I've always believed that the Lord has a sense of humour.... it was something I never envisaged, but the Lord blessed my time there.

It was when the possibility of working for Simon began to reveal itself, that I understood more about why the Lord had moved on the Education Authority, concerning the conditions they made in relation to what I would do after I'd finished my training. It really didn't make a great deal of sense that they paid my full teaching salary for a whole year - but didn't want anything in return. Isn't it amazing how Father can change things round? Only He knew that a year later Simon would need a sister in the Lord to work with him and encourage and support him in his business. We met every morning and shared business and personal information and often prayed together.

You might comment that it was a waste of my year of studying.... but the way the Lord looks at time is different than we do. I remember a dear brother, Arthur Burt for those who might know of him, saying to me back in the '70's that he'd just come back from a three day trip in Europe. And then went on to say that our God would send us any distance, even for a short time, if it meant Him drawing one of His lost sheep back into the fold. It never really surprised me after that, what He might ask me to do or where He might send me to do it, or for how long!

My First Experience of Grief

Do you remember me sharing in the previous chapter how, when I found out that my mother had cancer after my trip back to the UK in 1977, that I contacted all my friends and asked them to pray? I shared with you that as a result of that prayer, she lived for another five years. It was towards the end of the October, after I began working with Simon, that I planned a visit down to my parents in Folkestone - driving down on the Thursday and back on the Saturday to be at KCF on the Sunday.

Mum hadn't been feeling that great and that Thursday night was really rough - to the extent that Dad got the doctor in on Friday morning, who was able to give some pain relief. She didn't improve and, late that afternoon, was moved by ambulance to the William Harvey hospital in Ashford. Dad went in the ambulance and my brother, Chris who was living with them, drove up so he would be able to bring Dad back, when needed. I waited at home, praying for all three of them and placing them in Father's hands.

Around mid evening the phone rang and I thought it might be my father or brother letting me know how things were going. However, it was in fact the hospital. They explained that Dad and Chris, had been advised to go home, so were on the way - and then went on to say they were sorry, but my mother had passed away. In some ways, I appreciated the time on my own before they got home - and was able to talk out loud to my Father about it all and come to a place of accepting, with His help, what had happened. It did mean, though, that I had to break the news to them when they arrived home......

Next morning my Dad asked me if I could return a dress to a shop in town - one Mum had bought but not worn. I think he didn't know what to do with it and the thought of taking it back, or asking my brother to, was one step too far. I did, and it was as I was explaining 'why' to the shop assistant that I got rather 'wobbly'.... The men reckoned there was nothing else at that point that I could do and that it was probably sensible to keep to my plan to return to Surbiton later in the day. My brother had contacted my eldest sister, also living in Kent and my other sister and brother living in Australia and Tasmania respectively.

So I headed for home, but called in at Peter and Jean's first. They were out but Jean's Mum, who now lived there with them was there - and I shared the news with her. Her immediate reaction was to say "I believe she's with Jesus!"..... After the ambulance took Mum to the hospital, and I was praying - I had such a sense that she had moved to that place where she'd met with the Lord. This especially grew as I drove back up from Folkestone so, when Jean's Mum said what she did, it really witnessed in my spirit.

This belief, that my mother had met with Jesus and had actually gone to be with Him - was something that I had to stand in faith on, as nothing was said by her to confirm it before she passed away. I believe that she realised that she'd lived another 5 years through the power of prayer and had amazed the surgeon who had operated on her originally. I only found out afterwards that he'd seen her again not that long before she died - and couldn't believe she was still here. Our God is the God of the impossible. And sometimes, He gives us an assurance of

something that's happened in the spirit, that we cannot confirm except through believing it in faith, as there is no confirmation to actually see. I believe this is what happened concerning my mother getting to know Jesus.

I wonder what your experience of grief is - and how you handled it, or maybe even how you're handling it at the moment? I want to leave that question with you, and return to it later. What I will say is, that I'm aware with hindsight, that I never really grieved for my mother - and it's an area in our lives that we definitely need help from the Lord in coping with.....

God 'Links' in His Family

I need to go back briefly and give you more information on how I first got to know Jenny Reid and Margaret Matthews - two Irish girls who came over to England. They shared a flat in Kingston in the early '70's - and I got to know them when I visited KCF whilst living in Daventry. After I came back from Iran and was at the fellowship in the early '80's, we made contact again. Margaret had married and was then down in Southampton. Jenny had spent some time in Ipswich with Freda - and now was actually living at Tadworth, and at a fellowship in Cheam. Jenny was near enough to visit KCF and we met up again and got to know each other better.

Prayer and Worship Conferences

In the spring of '83 Jenny asked me to go to a Prayer and Worship Conference with her being held at Pilgrim Hall, a conference centre in Sussex - with Freda leading it. This was the first of these conferences to be held and I really believed that I should go. I am so thankful that I did as I found it such a blessing and I felt I learned so much. Later in the year there were two more - smaller in number, but such a blessing. It was so good to learn more about prayer and worship in a group and also to have the opportunity to get to know Freda better.

I'll share more about the conferences, and how the Lord used them over the years to create a 'family' from those who went on a regular basis, as I continue to share my story. They play a big part in my 'story', as do many of the 'family' that has been created through them.

I want to share something I learned at that first conference I went to at Pilgrim Hall, which I hadn't seen / realised before - something I've never forgotten, and has helped me through the years. In one of the sessions Freda said she felt from the Lord, that we should all stay as a group but, also, have time on our own to talk or listen to the Lord for ourselves. We were free to be quiet or pray aloud - whatever He laid on our heart to do.

After a little while a lady, not far from where I was sitting, began to weep - not gently, but what I would call 'deeply' and I was really moved by the way she was sobbing. This hadn't gone on for long before two other people went over to comfort her and put their arms round her. It was at that point I looked across at Freda and could see a sort of sadness in her face - almost a disappointment at what had happened.

At a later date I talked with Freda about what had happened with that lady. She confirmed what I'd begun to glimpse and

thought was the case - that there are times when we need to hold back from people upset in that way, and allow the Holy Spirit to minister to them, instead of giving them comfort ourselves. If we move in, unless of course the Lord tells us to, when we shouldn't, what we actually do is rob that person from an encounter with their Lord that He has engineered.

Quite a lengthy explanation - but one I felt the Lord wanted me to share with you. It is so important to realise that we can sometimes hinder, as well as help, people in their walk with Him.

Off to India at Last!

Earlier in my story I shared with you how the Lord spoke to me about going to India - it was early in '66, when I was at the children's home. I thought, at that time, that I would be going to live and work there in a 'mission' capacity. But, as you know, the Lord had other ideas and took me to Iran for three years instead. I also shared that it was 18 years, in fact, before He took me to India - yep, that's right, January '84! So I want to share with you how that came about....

At some stage in '83, I began to have thoughts stirring in me again about India. I've found that the Lord might sometimes start by giving me thoughts on something in particular that He's reminding me of - or even something completely new. I can't pinpoint anything that started them - just began to be aware they were there!

It got to the point when I felt I couldn't ignore my thoughts any longer and asked the Lord to show me any steps I should be taking to move towards it happening. I talked it over with Freda and found she had an Indian friend living not that far away from her - she suggested I spoke with her. The contact with Freda's friend resulted in an invite to visit her family in Delhi, when she visited them in January '84! Things were beginning to move.....

Around the same time the Lord brought me into contact with the New Frontier network of churches - and this covered both UK and overseas. I believe I went to one of their meetings, or even possibly a conference, and was chatting with someone about their connection with a New Frontiers church in Bombay (as it was then, now known as Mumbai) in India. They gave me contact details and suggested I write and talk to them about staying at their home in Bombay. Things were really moving now!

Venture of Faith

My visit to India for the month of January in '84 turned out to be a real venture of faith! I arranged with my boss Simon to take a month off work - and then I wrote to the couple in Bombay, Joe and Iris, introducing myself and giving dates etc. I booked my flight - before hearing back from them, as I was convinced this was what the Lord wanted me to move out on. I arranged with Freda's friend, Anita, to contact her when I got out there, with dates to go to Delhi.

The thing is, when I flew out from Heathrow - I hadn't heard back from Bombay! I had to trust the Lord that He'd got it covered. And, believe it or not - the same thing happened when I flew up to Delhi! It was certainly an adventure and definitely a venture of faith as well!

When I first arrived at Bombay airport there wasn't anyone to meet me. I just felt I should stay put and, in due course, someone turned up to collect me. And Delhi? Well there, I was going to wait inside - but felt a real check on that, so went out of the airport to wait. Praise the Lord - there was Anita waiting to meet me! God is so, so good.

I had a precious and memorable time in India - both in Bombay and Delhi. I met some lovely brothers and sisters in the Lord and was often overwhelmed by their openness and desire to share the Lord and everything they had. I would love to be able to share more of my time there - but maybe the Lord will have me do that another time!

What did I learn? A great deal - and I will try and share some of it with you....

For a start I was challenged and humbled by the openness and willingness to share their lives with a complete stranger - other than knowing that I loved the Lord as they did. Many of the people I met and spent time with were materially quite poor, compared to western standards, and yet were so rich in the Lord and in sharing all He had given them. It gave me an even greater desire to open my home and encourage the Body, than I already had.

The Lord underlined yet again that His timing is completely different to our concept of time. Looking back in the following years I knew it had been 18 yrs between His Word to me about going to India, and my visit there. But, when I went in January '84, that was obviously when I first realised the time gap - and it

was quite a shock, but thrilling at the same time! It made me look at 'timing' in connection with the Lord, in a completely different way from then onwards.

Of course, the other thing the Lord so underlined through the whole experience, was the safety in moving out into what He wants and shows us to do - when we trust Him. Sometimes He asks us to take big steps - such as I did in flying out to Bombay, when I hadn't actually heard anything back from Joe and Iris to say they were expecting me. But, more often, it's smaller steps and sometimes it's more difficult to take those than the big ones. In some ways, we'll dig deeper for faith to face the big things, but don't make so much effort for the smaller things.... but maybe that's just me. You'll have to ask yourselves that question....

One more out of the many things the Lord was teaching me - and one that I'm not free to give all the details of, but will share the outcome. I was put in a situation that I hadn't expected to meet, where someone challenged me on my attitude to something that I didn't feel was really true. The Lord was very gracious to me and helped me not to react but kept me calm, although I have to confess it hurt a bit and upset my feelings. Knowing what I know now and how clear the Word is on our not 'taking offence' - I realise that was a lesson that I actually only learned in part then, and have had to learn to go much deeper in, in the years since then.

In this instance I have shared the things I felt the Lord laid on my heart - I pray that as you read through them that Father will show you what He wants you to learn from them.

6/3 A Different Way of Life

Another Step - Another Reinforced Lesson

Walking with the Lord can be so exciting and unexpected at times - as long as we keep listening to the Holy Spirit! Around the beginning of the summer in '84 I started getting thoughts once more about teaching. They were accelerated when I learned that Hollyfield, the school where I'd previously been teaching, was looking for a part time teacher in the area of business studies - the subject I'd retrained to teach....

I made some enquiries at the school and found they would be interested in me returning there to be involved in, what would basically become eventually, a full blown Business Studies Department. Once again I was finding that, as I took a step forward in the direction I felt the Lord was showing me - so the following step started to be coming clearer. The next step, before I could go any further with the school, was to speak with Simon.

Simon realised that I wouldn't be moving in the direction I was, unless I believed that was what the Lord was showing me. He expressed the fact that he would miss me but wished me well in being obedient to the Lord. I knew I would miss him too, as I had really enjoyed working with him.

However, it was at this point I hit rather a 'glitch'. The first I was aware of this was when the main elder in the fellowship asked if I'd go and have a chat with him. KCF was led by a group of elders and the one who had asked to speak with me, was usually looked on as the leader.

We duly got together to talk. He explained that he felt that Simon still needed the help and encouragement that I gave to him in the work situation and, basically, asked me to reconsider what I was doing and stay where I was. It was a difficult situation, and a difficult and rather uncomfortable discussion. It also reminded me very much of the situation I'd found myself when in Iran, re my going up to Tehran to teach.

But I'm so glad that I'd had that experience, because it helped me to stand fast in the current situation, and have the courage to stick to what Father had shown me.

Once again I was in the situation of going against what someone in authority in my spiritual family, thought I should do. Like a great number of people, I don't like confrontational situations but, ultimately, I had to choose to be obedient to what the Lord showed me - or not. Looking back, I realise that Father was reinforcing the lesson that He first taught me in Iran. In some ways it was more difficult because I didn't move away, as before - but continued life where I was in Surbiton!

I continued, and still do, to believe we need to be held accountable to those the Lord puts over us to guide us - and the norm would be to heed the advice given. But, they too are human, and can make mistakes (just as much as I'm aware that I can), and ultimately we have to follow what Father says - not what man has said.....

I am realising and learning so much as I share my story with

you - and have just realised the preparation this gave me for events at a later stage in my life. Will share - further on!

A New Role at Hollyfield

Having made the necessary decisions, followed by applying for the new post back at Hollyfield school - things began to move forward. Interviews and paperwork were all completed and I was due to start at the beginning of the autumn term in the September of '84. I finished working with Simon and enjoyed a bit of a break before I started back at school. I'm glad to say that we remained good friends.

It was a part-time post (3 days) that I had at Hollyfield this time round. Most schools by then were venturing in to the IT scene and eventually into Business Studies - and Hollyfield was no exception. So, the majority of my classes in my first year back at the school, were linked to IT and the practical skills involved. The main practical knowledge that was needed was learning key board skills, and these were mainly taught on manual typewriters - which certainly don't make an appearance in schools today!

Alongside these basic practical skills I was also teaching basic computer skills in classes which numbered 20 students, with 10 computer stations, which were shared - two youngsters per station.... The computers were the original BBC B's made by Acorn which made their way into a large number of schools in the mid '80's. Through the year we covered word processing, databases and spreadsheets - spending one term on each. I don't know about my students, but it was definitely a learning curve for me!

I was fully aware that some of the youngsters already knew more than I did at that point. Mind you it came in handy sometimes - especially when, for example, I had no idea how to put another roll of paper on the printer (a roll that fitted on the sprockets)..... I was so thankful to the Lord that one of the boys showed me how and fitted it for me!

On my return to Hollyfield, there were still quite a number of students who knew me from when I taught there previously. My original thoughts from when I was considering changing from RE to teach business studies, came back to me. I found that they were in fact correct, and I did have more opportunity to share the Lord - and more openness in the receiving! Initially some of it came from being asked why I changed and whether I now no longer believed in God. But I actually found the openness continued, even after those initial questions had been asked.

By the time I was in my second year back at school, the subject of business studies in schools began to expand and I became involved in teaching the extra areas that were being added.

After being back in 'office' life, and working with someone with whom I could share Jesus and know I'd be understood - it was quite challenging to be back working in a school scenario. Also in the job I'd come from, I'd had a fair amount of authority and responsibility for others I worked with. Completely different to being back and teaching in school.

But I do believe that whenever the Lord moves us into something new and/or different - He will always equip us to accomplish there what He has on His heart for us to do. And

that's what happened - and He began to show me what else He had in mind for me.....

Other Changes Outside of Teaching

Alongside the changes taking place in my working life, there were other changes happening in my personal life.

When I got back from Iran, and was living in Surbiton and part of the fellowship there, I'd felt it important to get to know as many people as I could. There were a number that I'd already known for a number of years, but knew it was important not just to spend time with them only.... When I started to teach part time I was thrilled because it meant there was more time to spend with others in the fellowship and help and encourage them in their walk with the Lord. I found this especially the case with the young mums with young children.

I believe as a community of God's people we should support and encourage each other in every way possible - basically we are God's Family and need to function in the same way as a normal family would.

My friend Jenny, who took me with her to the first Prayer and Worship conference in the early part of '83, went off to New Zealand later that year and spent the winter of '83/'84 out there. On her return in the spring - she came and joined me in Surbiton and we shared the flat there for the next three years. I'd been living on my own since I'd come back from Iran and, just as I'd had to learn to live on my own - I now had to learn to share again! Actually, we made a good team as she worked full time in the fellowship - and I worked part time....

After the first few years instead of there being 2, or even occasionally 3, of the conferences - it became an annual event during the week following the August bank holiday. We met in the Salvation Army Conference Centre at Sunbury-on-Thames briefly but, by '87 we moved and met at High Leigh, a conference centre at Hoddesdon in Hertfordshire. The positioning of this was more central for folk coming from both the north and south of the country - and there we stayed! I missed the conference early in the year of '84, due to not being back from India in time, as the first one that year was held in early February. But missed very few in the years following.... As I believe I mentioned earlier - the Prayer and Worship conferences, with so many of us going on a regular basis, became very much a family and we looked forward to catching up with one another each year, as many of us lived very far apart. I never came away from a conference without feeling that I'd been so blessed and challenged, and that I'd been taken deeper into my relationship with Jesus - and that was as well as the sheer joy of being together with those I loved in the presence of the Lord.

The three years that Jenny and I were sharing the flat in Surbiton, were ones in which I felt I was learning more all the time and going deeper in my walk with the Lord. As I've said before - I believe we need those around us who are further on in their relationship with the Lord, in order that we might be challenged and learn more ourselves. All of us need to have the desire to grow deeper in our love relationship with Jesus and, very often, it takes the challenges of those around us to help us to do

that.

One example I can give particularly - I found Jenny had gone deeper in the realm of speaking in tongues and possessed a greater knowledge and understanding in that area than I felt I had. She had spent some time living in Ipswich with Freda - and she had learned and grown in her relationship with the Lord at that time. I felt, during my time of sharing the flat with Jenny, I learned and went deeper with Jesus......

A New Adventure and Way of Life

Into my second year of being back teaching at Hollyfield there came another opportunity for a new venture, which didn't entail leaving the school, but did open up a new area that I'd not thought about previously. This was getting involved in the Adult Education that was taking place within Kingston's Education Authority. Just as business studies was growing in schools as a specified subject, it was an area that was also growing and needing classes amongst adults due to the new technology expanding in the business world.

I started teaching some Adult Education classes, initially mainly word processing, but then also sessions on databases and spread sheets - similar to what I was doing in school. I began to realise just how wide spread the need for this training amongst adults was required. That's when I first began to think about finishing school completely, becoming self-employed and setting up my own business! The desire to do this began to grow in me and, once again, I found myself in the position where I needed to take a step forward and trust the Lord to show me what to do next.

Actually in a way, I suppose I took two steps in one - I started the process of registering as a self-employed business and getting the paperwork completed, etc; and, at the same time, I handed my notice in at school....

I felt the Lord showed me the next step quite quickly. I realised that I'd need some extra income, until I was more established - with people wanting to employ me in the realm of business training and doing accounts for other small businesses; and got myself a job as a 'temp'. I had worked as a 'temp' before I went to college back in '66 - working on payrolls. This time round it was word processing - and I had such a laugh with the Lord, as I was sent to work in the offices of Kingston Education Authority!

I also continued to teach in Adult Education classes and added book keeping to the ones that I taught; alongside all day intensive courses in setting up and using spreadsheets. Actually, I found that there were often people in the various classes I taught, and especially in the case of word processing, who wanted to go further in their training. When they realised that I also taught privately, I found myself employed by them on a one-to-one basis. I would say that most of the people I worked for on that basis knew of me by 'word of mouth', as I didn't really advertise. Another area I did some work in was 'proof reading'. And I never dreamed of the use the Lord would make of that at a later stage in my life - which I will share with you at the appropriate time.

It was the July of '86 that I left Hollyfield and worked as a 'temp' for a few weeks, before officially becoming self-employed. This left me with even greater freedom than when I worked part-time, as I was able to have the 'say-so' of when I worked and when I spent time with people in the fellowship.

I've possibly said this before, or something similar.... that it's so important not to get too entrenched in what we're doing and begin to think 'that's it' and that's where we'll stay. I believe, as the Lord's people and His representatives here on earth, that we really do need to be open to the leading of the Holy Spirit. We basically need to be willing to go, to be and to do - anything that He shows us to - plus being willing to stay put where we are, as sometimes that's as much, or even more, of a challenge than moving elsewhere! How else is His Kingdom going to grow unless we're willing to let Him show us what He wants done - and then are obedient?

More Change Arriving!

In the summer of '87 Jenny was invited to visit friends in the States - a couple who used to be in KCF but now lived in Florida. She felt that on her return she should spend some time with her Mum who lived in Bushey, the other side of London, near to Watford, and who hadn't been too well. This actually became a permanent move for her, and she got a position as an Occupational Therapist over there, which was the area she was professionally trained in!

Once again I was on my own in the flat and continued with my self employed work, plus teaching my Adult Education classes; plus the contact with folk in the fellowship.

Unfortunately, it was around that time that KCF, as it had

been, more or less came to an end. This isn't the place, and certainly not in my remit, to relate what took place and obviously, if it was only my comments that you read here - it would be much too one sided. I feel that's all I can say really....

It's sad when break ups in church fellowships happen, and I'm sure it saddens Father most of all, but ultimately our responsibility is to get up and continue our relationship and walk with Jesus.

What Next?

I continued to fellowship when possible with those I was in contact with. Also, I had the bonus of my High Leigh 'family' and continued to go to the Prayer and Worship conference each year. It was at High Leigh that I got to know Clive and Lynne better, from Seaforth church at New Malden - not far from where I was at Surbiton! Little did I realise this was another 'God connection' that He would develop in due course.....

When I look back now, it amazes me the amount that the Lord packed into my life in those years in Surbiton through the '80's!

I believe that one of the main, overall lessons the Lord began to teach me, after He turned the tide in my life, was not to be so dependent on other people and be more dependent on Him. As I've said previously, I believe it's important that we walk with one another together with the Lord in His family - but so important not to become more dependent on our brothers and sisters, than on Him.

I was fully aware of the potential in me to do that, and so grateful that Father put me with those who wouldn't let me be dependent on them, and loved me enough to challenge me about it if they needed to.....

In those years in Surbiton I believe the Lord took me further and deeper in being dependent only on Him.

CHAPTER 7

Relocation and Following God

7/1 Maureen – a New Family and a New Season

Spreading My Wings

Something happened at High Leigh that was the first step in another direction that the Lord started to take me on. I shared with you earlier how Clive and Lynne, from Seaforth Church at New Malden where in fact Clive was the Pastor, had started coming to High Leigh and I had got to know them. At High Leigh in '89 we sat together one lunchtime, and Clive was sharing with those of us at the table that, in a few weeks time, they were having their church weekend away - to be held at Wycliffe Bible College. He also said they were a bit concerned that, so far they had no one to spend time with the children - to give them some 'fun' time, but also some time learning more about Jesus.

Do you ever experience those times when someone is sharing something - and suddenly you get a nudge in your spirit and you know the Holy Spirit wants you to listen carefully and, more often than not, it's something you need to take some action over! Well..... that's exactly what happened when Clive was speaking.....

The trouble was - I didn't really want to listen to what Clive was saying, as I was pretty sure already that it was going to involve offering to go and work with the children over their church weekend; and I wasn't particularly enthusiastic, especially as I didn't know any of the children either. I ended up asking him and Lynne more about what they envisaged for the children's sessions - and said I'd ask the Lord about it. I knew I had to ask and be willing, as I knew I'd lose my peace otherwise.....

Yes, I did ask the Lord about it - and yes, before we left High Leigh to go home I shared with Clive and Lynne that I'd be willing to do the children's sessions for them at their weekend away. I also said I'd join them on the following Sunday for the morning service - and that, in a nutshell, is how I started to attend Seaforth Church; because I began going on a regular basis after that! It was good to meet the folk there, and especially some of the children, prior to the weekend away.

Jenny and I kept in close contact, although she was no longer at the flat but living with her Mum, and she agreed to come and give me a hand for the weekend at Wycliffe, which was a great help. It was good to have the opportunity to get to know everyone better whilst we were there.

Have you realised that the Holy Spirit is so often gentle in His dealings with us - with me, and with you? We always have a choice as to whether we listen/accept His nudges about things He's highlighting to us with a view to us being obedient to what He wants us to do.....

In the situation I've just shared - I wasn't pushed into saying yes, but the Holy Spirit lovingly brought me to the point of being willing to. Once we choose to be obedient, He gives us all the help we need to accomplish the task He sets before us - we're not left to just get on with it on our own!

The weekend away was good and I felt that I'd begun to make new friends - both with the adults and the young people.

First Real Contact

There was a lady at Seaforth, called Maureen, who brought her two youngest children, John and Helen, to the church every week. We began to get to know each other and I invited them to the flat for lunch on a Sunday at the beginning of December '89 - I remember the timing of it as it was just before Jenny and I went off to Malta on holiday for a week! It wasn't too cold, although it was December, and we had a walk along the river towards Kingston in the afternoon, as it was at the end of the road where I lived.

We obviously saw each other at church but the next specific time we got together was during the school half-term in the following February. John and Helen had gone down to Bridgwater in the West Country to stay with one of their older sisters, and Maureen said she was feeling quite strange without them being around, as it was the first time they'd been old enough to travel down there on the coach on their own, but supervised by the bus company. We drove up to the Isabella Plantation in Richmond Park, very near to Kingston, where there were some beautiful gardens - plus somewhere nice to have tea! Afterwards, before I dropped her home, I said to Maureen that if she wanted to talk any time, to just feel free to ring me whenever she wanted to.....

Well, and we often laughed at this in the years following, she did ring me - every day for a week, just to find out if I'd really meant what I said! I believe Maureen had gone through some difficult relationships previously, which resulted in her having difficulty in trusting people as to whether they really meant what they said.

People in the church, those who wanted to, were paired up with someone each month in order to pray regularly together. Lynne asked me if I would be happy to be paired with Maureen for the next month - which would be March '90. She also, as tactfully as she could, suggested I go gently as Maureen could at times be 'a bit fiery', if she was upset by people..... I paused for a moment or two, and then found myself saying (and I believe this was what the Lord gave me to say) - I said that "If I go when the Lord shows me to go - then there won't be any difficulties, because He will have gone ahead and prepared the way." I didn't know when I said that, to what extent Father had done just that -

prepared the way. You'll understand when I share with you what took place - which I'll do as we go forward with my story.

I believe I shared with you in the first chapter how the Lord taught me to live one day at a time - and that it's something I've found so valuable and continued to do ever since, for over fifty years now! I obviously did plan ahead and have some idea of what I'd be doing, especially as I continued to work on a self-employed basis at this time. But I was also always aware, and still am, that I needed to be open to the fact that Father might have something different on His heart for me to do - and I should be prepared to make changes if that was how the Holy Spirit led me on any particular day.

I want to encourage you to always be open to anything the Lord may show you to do, that is different to what you might have planned. In other words - don't have every day 'set in stone' but be flexible as the Holy Spirit leads you.....

God Connections

Now I'd like to share with you what happened when I went to see Maureen about meeting up through March to pray together. It wasn't something I'd arranged beforehand - I really did go on the day that Father prompted me to and, because I believe it was very much His timing, I soon realised that He'd given a greater freedom in sharing with one another than we'd had previously. I explained why I had come, but also why I hadn't made any specific arrangement - because I felt it so important to be meeting up when God had planned it, not when we had.

We shared various things about our individual experiences in our personal journey with Jesus through the years and, yes, I did share with her the suicide attempt and how God had stepped in and saved me. Then Maureen shared something that really excited me and made me realise how important it had been that I'd listened to the Holy Spirit's prompting and gone to see her when I did in response to His prompting. And this is what she shared with me.....

She said she'd been going through a hard time, and this was particularly so because she felt she didn't really make contact with other believers - primarily because they didn't seem to understand her relationship with the Lord, and therefore didn't understand what she shared about her experience. She explained that she had come to know the Lord as a teenager when she first attended Seaforth church many years before. She'd been married twice and had 4 children in each marriage - her first husband turned out to be an alcoholic and her second physically abused her and her children.

It was during her second marriage, whilst living in Royston in Hertfordshire, that she gradually came back into a relationship with Jesus - which is what enabled her to cope. She wasn't able to attend a church because of the difficulties at home. Eventually her doctor said that her husband (second) would have to leave the marital home, otherwise he would have to arrange for the children to go into care. Her husband left and also, not long afterwards, her father passed away and, to cut a long story short, Maureen bought the half of his house that would have been her sister's, and moved the family back to New Malden, although some of the older ones at that point stayed in Royston. On her own now, she made contact once again with Seaforth church and started going there on a regular basis.

The difficulty she felt she faced, arose from the fact that her relationship with Jesus was very close and on a one-to-one basis - which was what had enabled her to come through the traumatic time of her second marriage and the eventual breakdown of it that happened. You see, she didn't feel that others understood the relationship she had with Jesus and, the evening prior to the day that I felt the Lord said I should go and see her...... she had cried out in desperation to the Lord - asking Him if there was anyone who would understand, and who talked to the Lord in the way that she did!

It was so encouraging when Maureen shared with me the question that she had asked the Lord about the night before, and it so resonated in my spirit! Her experience in finding a place in her love relationship with Jesus, to cope with the trauma of the circumstances of her second marriage - felt very similar to my own experience in coping after the suicide attempt that I had made. It gave me an understanding of what she was saying, which I don't think I would have been able to have had otherwise.....

On the Move Again

Over the weeks following we met up quite a lot and learned more about what had happened in our lives previously, and I also got to know John (youngest son - 9) and Helen (youngest daughter - 11). Aaron the next son up, who was 16, was in the process of going into the army. It was John who seemed quite concerned about me driving up from Surbiton to visit them in New Malden - and also to attend church on a Sunday, although it was only around 10 or so minutes, unless the traffic was really bad. The next thing we knew - he was suggesting that I leave my flat and move in with them!

Actually, Maureen told me afterwards that she'd had the same thought, although felt it would be better if either John or Helen suggested it. If it came from them they couldn't say that she had forced them to accept me into the family..... It was Father's wisdom, actually as, when I met the older children (adults already) later at Terry's wedding - it took some time before I was accepted!

Yep, you guessed correctly - I did move in with Maureen and the family, although I kept the flat until August. This was simply because a friend was staying there and my landlady agreed that she could stay until she was able to move on to her new accommodation. I sorted out what I needed to keep, gave away things I didn't need to - and Maureen helped me clean it up ready to hand back to my landlady. I'd been based there for roughly 11 1/2 years, so it was quite a change.

We then went off to the conference at High Leigh; whilst John and Helen once again went down to Somerset to stay with family. It was Maureen's first time at High Leigh, although she knew all about it because she would normally look after Clive and Lynne's two children, whilst they were there. And I'd shared a fair amount about it as well! She'd also already met Iolo and Freda when she'd been up to Barmouth to help with the work on the house during Easter, earlier in the year. It was a 'full house' that year and we ended up sleeping in my camper van..... Maureen soon became part of the High Leigh family, and we continued going together in the following years.

I settled in with my new 'family' in New Malden - more adjustments as it wasn't just another adult, but children involved as well, for the first time since I'd been at the Hostel in Isfahan in Iran. So for both Maureen and myself it was a new season of our lives that we were entering into. I continued with my self-employed work in business studies, plus continuing to teach Adult Education classes. Maureen worked part-time for a local Christian firm producing Christian magazines and a newspaper as well, I believe.

At the risk of the probability that I'm repeating myself - I really can't say often enough, the importance that we ALWAYS need to remain open to the leading of the Holy Spirit, and be willing to listen to any changes He might want to make in our lives. And also point out, that it doesn't just apply to outward changes in our lives and circumstances. It also applies just as much to what's going on inside of us - the way we behave towards people and our attitude in different situations, not to mention the importance of what we think and say.....

We should never think ourselves too old, or to have come far enough along our journey with the Lord to think that there are no longer things to be changed in our lives. As I believe I've said before - we're not likely to reach that point where there is nothing that needs dealing with..... not, that is, until He takes us home to glory!

Moving On....

After we came back from High Leigh we began to realise that it looked as though there was going to be another change ahead. Maureen's three older girls were based in Bridgwater, Somerset - and it seemed that the Lord might be moving us down in that direction also.....

What can I say? For me it was the second move in less than a year - something that I've only just realised as I'm sharing this with you now! But, in spite of it being so soon after my move to New Malden, it just seemed so right and I was at peace and, actually, excited about it! Excited at what the Lord had in store for us, and excited too at the thought of living in a country town rather than in the outer area of London!

7/2 Off to the West Country

Our First God Connection

On Saturday, the day after High Leigh ended (first Saturday in September '90) we headed off to Bridgwater - mainly to pick up John and Helen, but also to see the other members of the family living there. We joined the Community Church in Bridgwater for the morning meeting on the Sunday. This was partly in order to be able to meet Ken Ford, the leader of the fellowship at that time, whom Maureen had already had contact with by phone and spoken to regarding her concern about one of her daughters in Bridgwater. He'd very kindly met her daughter and prayed for her, and she wanted to thank him in person. When we eventually moved to Bridgwater at the beginning of May '91 - this was the church we believed the Lord wanted us to join....

This was another situation where we had a growing conviction in our spirits that we needed to start acting on the 'pull' we seemed to be getting towards Bridgwater! The first step we took was to see what was available on the housing market, so we made enquiries - first through looking at the local papers, which Maureen's daughters posted to us; and then details of houses from the estate agents, which we requested to be posted to us.

What were we doing? We were moving out in faith and acting on the little we knew - and trusting the Lord would show us more as we took each step forward..... and He did! Hallelujah!

House Hunting

Our move to Bridgwater in May '91 was the first of five moves that the Lord took us on during the time I shared with Maureen - the last being in January 2011, and where I continue to live today, without any sense that I'm likely to move again. Although I do have to put a proviso on that - as far as I know at the moment I won't move again, unless.... 'yes' I would if I believed Father wanted me to. Two of the moves were in West Somerset, where we moved to in January '93; then back to Bridgwater in November '2005, and the final move I've already mentioned, to where I live currently. I live on my own now as Maureen went to be with the Lord in 2014, as some of you may have realised. But, once again, I'm getting ahead of myself!

Each of our moves were adventures with the Lord, though not without challenges. I would love to share in more detail but, as I said about my time in Iran (Chapter 5/3), it isn't in my remit to do so here.... I'm aware that it's important that what I share in this book is what Father lays on my heart to share; although I'm not ruling out the possibility of future books to share the story with you!

I trust, having read through as far as this, that you are understanding of the fact that the desire of my heart is to be obedient to what my Father shows me to do. I gradually realised and knew that through the way that He stepped in and saved my life and 'turned the tide' (remember the choice I made at the 'crossroads' to go on with Him) - I knew that I could never be a free agent again, in as much as I always want to walk with Him,

and not go my own way.....

Working

Whilst we were still in Bridgwater in the early '90's, Maureen mainly worked at Oak Trees, a Care Home, as a Night Superviser. I spent the first few months temping in a firm's accounts department, before going as a Supply teacher to Kingsmead School in Wiviliscombe, which was situated the other side of Taunton, the county town of Somerset. I'd been asked to go there as an RE teacher as they were having difficulty recruiting one. I was, in due course, asked to stay on as Head of the RE Department and was there for a couple of years. In some ways it was strange to be teaching RE again and also to be teaching full time!

I continued to work there for a time when we moved out to Watchet in West Somerset, but Maureen left Oak Trees and looked for something more local. She initially worked for a private firm and later worked in the Care section of Social Services in Somerset.

I finished teaching in the summer of '93, and actually was out of work for about 3 years during which time the Job Centre decided I was too old at 50, and too qualified.... and I am grateful to the Lord for having given me a sense of humour. Then, in the October of '96 I got a job as an Admin Assistant for the Youth Service, Somerset County - 12 hrs based in Watchet initially. In due course I had another 6hrs added which were based in Minehead - and eventually another 6hrs were added and I ended up back in Watchet on 24 hrs. Moves were made within the Youth Service and new accommodation found for our work base. I actually worked for the Youth Service for ten years, until I retired in 2006; by which time we were living back in Bridgwater!

Actually, after the break I'd had from teaching in school for a few years - I enjoyed being back in the classroom. Looking back at that time - it almost seems as though the Lord was highlighting to me the fact that He really had known what He was doing when He took me into teaching, even though I'd not been very keen initially! Likewise with the office based side of work that He took me into and, when I retrained to teach business studies, it was almost as though He'd combined the two together....

So what did I learn from the working experience in my life during this time? I believe I learned, in a very practical way, to what extent Father understands us and plans out our lives in love to fulfil the needs that each one of us have. I've also learned what a very practical Father we have - that He wants the best for us, not just in the 'spiritual' area of our life, but in the practical every day stuff that goes to make up the way we live as we walk with Him each day.

Family Life

I need to catch you up on 'family' life during this time....

When we moved to Watchet Helen, Maureen's youngest daughter, ended up staying in Bridgwater with Claire - Maureen's eldest daughter. Aaron, the son who had moved out not long before I joined the family; came down to join us, not long before we moved to Watchet - at which time he got digs and a job in Bridgwater.

So it was only John who moved with us out to Watchet, until he went into the Army in the September of '97. All Maureen's daughters plus Aaron, were living in Bridgwater - with Terry, the next son up from Aaron, living with his wife and children up in Hounslow. Paul, her eldest son, was still up in Hertfordshire, until he sadly passed away in November '97.

I think you would agree that family life for everyone, whether it's very good or, at the other end of the scale, very difficult, is always eventful - in some form or another. And the family Father had put me in for this season I'm currently sharing about with you here - wasn't any different! But remember - we are never alone in the difficulties and challenges we face, and the Lord sees us through every single one of them.....

I'd like to share with you a hard challenge that we went through from May onwards to October '97 in connection with Maureen's health. She'd not been feeling so well in the March / April time and the doctor referred her to a consultant at Musgrove Park hospital in Taunton. After investigation, which involved having a colonoscopy, we were told that she appeared to have bowel cancer. They thought it had reached Stage B and she would need major surgery to remove as much of the cancer as possible - but weren't certain, until they operated, whether it would result in having a permanent colostomy or just a temporary one. Things happened pretty swiftly and they took Maureen in for her operation about the middle of July.

As soon as we knew what was happening, we contacted as many of our High Leigh family as possible and asked them to pray; plus all our other friends we knew who loved the Lord and would also pray..... When the operation took place the surgeons found that the cancer was not so far advanced and was at Stage A - not B. We believed that the Lord reversed the stage in answer to prayer. They found it hadn't gone to any other part of Maureen's body, although it was too far down on the colon to be able to reverse the colostomy at a later date. Amazingly she was back at work in the October!

In November of 2005 we moved back into Bridgwater - mainly, I believe, to be nearer the family. The grandchildren were growing up and moving towards the time when they'd be having children of their own!

God has a heart for His children, His family, and that's us, you and me, to live in unity - and that's what He desires that our earthly families should also portray. His intention, and desire, is that our earthly family should be modelled on our spiritual family ie the church Body.

The challenge, both for you and for myself, is that we walk with Jesus and live our lives in such a way that we portray Him - and draw others to want to walk with Him....

Fellowship Through These Years

I shared earlier how, when we first moved to Bridgwater we became part of the Community Church there, prior to moving out to West Somerset, and this was our initial contact with God's family in Somerset.

During those years we were in West Somerset we met up with several different sections of God's family - some of whom knew each other, some of them didn't. The contact ranged from the Baptist Church in Watchet to the Elim Church in Minehead and included a sizeable group that met in a hall in Carhampton, and a small group meeting in a home in Minehead! The Lord seemed to take us to them - to use us in the way He wanted - and then move us out again.

The eight years back in Bridgwater together, before the Lord took Maureen home - weren't quite so widespread, though no less eventful! Father took us into the then Pentecostal Church (AOG) in Bridgwater and we were there for a couple of years making a number of new friends. At the point in time when He took us out again - another small group, several of them from the Pentecostal Church among them whom we knew quite well, had started meeting together on a Sunday evening. Through the remaining years Maureen and I were together, we joined them as and when the Lord took us - and they were gracious enough to always make us welcome.....

What I've shared with you may possibly sound rather strange and, in some respects, it does to me as well. But I can only share what we experienced and what we felt the Lord led us to do - although some of it we didn't (and I still don't) necessarily understand, and have had to trust the One Who does understand and leave it with Him.....

I think that sometimes we feel we should know and understand all that the Lord is doing in our lives - but where would our need to trust and walk in faith come in, if we knew and could see where everything fitted in? Something for you to ponder on and talk to Father about.....

Fellowship at Barmouth (Mid-Wales)

So as not to confuse you, I need to share with you how Barmouth comes into this equation! My dear friend Freda married again in '86 - and I should also explain that her first husband went to be with the Lord in '79. Iolo, the man she married, had a large house on the promenade at Barmouth and the Lord gave them a vision of it being used for small groups gathering together for ministry - especially 'married couples' and (separately needless to say!) 'singles'. This would be alongside the continuing ministry through the 'Prayer and Worship' conferences at High Leigh and their trips to various other countries to minister.

It was an old property and needed quite a lot of work to bring it to the point of being suitable for groups to be able to stay. Various members in the Body were able to offer their help in accomplishing the work; and over the next few years this took place. A final 'push' as it were, took place over the Easter holiday period in 1990 and quite a number of folk came to help for as long as they were able to. I went up for those three weeks to cook for all those who came and stayed - I had been previously, but had been working on the house at that point. Maureen came up to help as well for a few days over the actual Easter weekend.

The first of the groups was held later in the summer of that year, and I again had the privilege of cooking for the married couples that came. Through the following years (18 I believe) there were different groups held there - quite often two groups following each other with one for couples and one for singles. Maureen and I had the privilege of going together to cook on several occasions, mainly in the first half of those years. And we went to one of the singles groups (so we weren't cooking that time) in the summer of 2008 and were really blessed! Actually, that year saw the last of the groups held at Barmouth, and we felt so glad that we'd been able to go.....

It was such a privilege to have been involved to some extent in what the Lord was doing at Barmouth - and when we weren't physically there we were able to continue to pray! We were involved in feeding the physical bodies of those who came; but also joined as many sessions as we were able to as well. We always left for home aware of having been fed spiritually.....

Fellowship at the Prayer and Worship Conferences

When we moved to the West Country Maureen and I made doubly sure that we went up to the conferences, although there were a few years in the mid '2000's' that we were unable to get there. As I've already shared with you, they were very much our 'Family' and gave us really, a continuity of fellowship and support that we needed through those years. We knew that, if there was a difficult decision that we faced and weren't completely clear on, we could ring and ask Freda to pray. I didn't need to give her the details - just say that we needed a Word from the Lord. It is so, so valuable to have friends like her!

The High Leigh conference continued annually through to 2011, though sadly without Iolo as He went to be with the Lord in 2003. In May of that year of 2011 Father took Freda home. Anita, Freda's daughter, led a team consisting of John and Elisabeth Plummer, Clive and Lynne Jones, Gill Bough and with Meredith (Iolo's son) continuing to look after the 'sound' - and the conference was able to go ahead. Since that time the conference was held bi-annually until the pandemic arrived and the 2021 conference was unable to be held. Some of the 'team' have stepped aside now, and as yet the Lord hasn't revealed the way forward, or whether now is the time for them to finish. But, praise God - Father knows!

I believe only our Father is fully aware of what has been accomplished for His Kingdom through the years and there will be many who will testify in Glory of how they were helped to grow in their relationship with the Lord, through attending the conferences. All I know is that I'm one of them and Maureen was also. Our fellowship, in and through the conferences, was particularly an anchor for us through these years in the West Country and I'm so thankful to the Lord, I know we both were.

7/3 Power of Praise

Is Praise Important?

Is praise important to you in your walk and relationship with the Lord?

Back in Ch 4/2 I shared a bit about how I was learning more about praising the Lord, and that it was particularly emphasised and portrayed to me through the time I spent in Daventry, when I first became part of the family with Peter and Jean. To save you searching back to find what I said... here is some of it to remind you: "I began to learn and understand more about praising God in all that's happening in our lives on a day to day basis - not just when we gather with other believers in a meeting. I could see the difference it made in the way Peter and Jean lived their lives, when they always had thanks and praise on their lips - whether they felt like it or not."

I also shared: "In Psalm 34:1 it says "I WILL bless the Lord at all times; His praise shall continually be in my mouth." David encourages us to do this - he found it worked and wanted others to know as well." Praise isn't an airy fairy thing - we're taught in the Word that it's what we should be doing. We also read in the Old Testament of how the Lord would command the kings to send the 'singers' out in front of their armies as part of their battle plans.

You see there is power in the praise we give to our King!!

Why? It's because it's a weapon we can use against the enemy - you don't find satan hanging around when you start to praise the Lord.... In fact, years ago, we used to sing a song with the words in it: "His praise is our battle cry"!

Through the years I learned more about praise and worship, but I don't think I began to fully realise the power there is in praise, until I was faced with a particular situation in my life.

I've shared before how that, as we go forward in our walk and relationship with the Lord, we might sometimes wonder why we seem to be taught pretty much the same lesson(s) over again. But I believe that, every time we face a familiar lesson, we are actually being taken deeper into a working knowledge of that lesson. And I believe that's what happened with me learning more about praise and going deeper in that knowledge. As I write this I've been reminded how, when out in Germany and recovering from the suicide attempt - one of the things I started doing was walking out in the country and singing hymns/songs I knew, especially "Great is Thy faithfulness". What was I doing? I was praising God and it was very much part of my healing at that time - which I'm only starting to understand all these years later....

Dear friends - please never under estimate the power of praise in your lives!

Discovering the Power of Praise

It was on the May Day Bank Holiday of 2014 that we realised that Maureen was ill - alerted by her sinking into a coma induced by a very low sugar level, which resulted in having to call an ambulance. The paramedics administered sugar into her blood stream and this revived her, but they advised seeing her doctor asap! This was the start of a very difficult journey, as various tests and scans took place and, on 16th of June, Maureen was told she had a very aggressive form of terminal cancer, with a large growth on her liver with only a few months to live.

This isn't the place to go into great detail about those last months before she went to be with Lord early in September. We alerted the High Leigh family once again, and all our friends who loved the Lord, to pray - just as we had back in '97 when she had bowel cancer. This cancer wasn't in any way connected with the bowel cancer and she'd been clear for 17 years. But this time Father didn't step in – not in the same way. By the middle of July we had a hospital bed in the lounge and Maureen was virtually immobile - apart from being helped to stand and then being able to move a few steps. Quite soon she was also in need of oxygen to help with her breathing. She wasn't well enough to cope with chemotherapy, so really it was a case of helping her to be as comfortable as possible.

Maureen was able to stay at home, although we needed help from carers coming in. She didn't cope very well with hospitals - in spite of (or maybe because of) having been a nursing auxiliary when younger! So you see Father was very gracious in allowing that - and we were both so thankful to Him.

I have to be honest and say that I didn't find it very easy to praise in the early days of those months, when everything seemed to happen so quickly. Then one day, as I was walking down to Morrisons supermarket to pick up some shopping, I suddenly found myself singing some words of a song that I'd learned many years before - in the '70's I think. It had been so long since I'd sung it that I couldn't remember all of it, but what I did remember was "My God, has the world at His command, Why should I fear?...." It so stirred my spirit and I can't begin to tell you what a difference that made...... and I did gradually remember the other words over time. I wouldn't be able tell you how many times I sung that song through those challenging months.

Once I'd started singing and praising again - I began remembering more of the older songs from the '70's and '80's, many of them based on scripture and fairly short. God is so faithful. I realised that, if I was going to be of any help to Maureen through these last months of her life, I needed to be in a place of victory over my emotions - and I was realising that the only way that could happen was to lean in close to Jesus, allow Him to lift me above my emotions and use the power there was in praise to shift the enemy out of the equation!

I'm not saying I was on top all the time - there were many times I'd 'go down' and need to praise my way up again through tears and raw emotion of all that was happening. But I especially asked the Lord for His strength to help Maureen through the difficult time she was facing. We both believed death is not the end when you know and love the Lord, and we were heading for eternity - but getting past the 'physical death' bit isn't always easy!

As I look back at that last summer when Maureen was so ill, I'm so grateful to the Lord for what He was teaching me about the power of praise - and in such a practical way. I don't know about you, but I'm someone who learns more easily, and grasps

things so much better, when I learn in a practical setting by 'doing'. And in this instance it was definitely a case of learning by doing! I know, without any doubt, that I learned more about the power of praise because I was in circumstances where I had to put it into practice. And I also know I wouldn't have survived in the situation, without learning what I needed to..... God is so good.

I would encourage you to face the challenges of the circumstances that Father takes you through. Face them and trust Him for the help you need to go 'through' them - rather than looking for and even asking for a way to escape from them. Going through them will be part of the way He equips you in your walk with Him to be able to accomplish all He has planned for you!

Maureen Goes Home

I shared earlier that Father took Maureen home in the early part of September 2014 - what I didn't say was that it was on the eighth day, which was actually the day before her 74th birthday. The enemy 'made hay' out of that, as Birthday and Sympathy cards came pretty well together in the same post - but, with Father's help, I managed not to let it 'get' to me.....

Those first days were pretty hectic as you can probably imagine; and in many ways that was a help in itself - I had to get on with all the things that needed doing. These ranged from returning all the drugs in the house to the pharmacy and getting all the hospital equipment collected; notifying everybody what had happened; through to registering Maureen's death officially; and much more besides.

With so much to do, it didn't allow me a great deal of time to dwell on being in the house on my own. But, it was during those first days that I began to realise all over again - I wasn't on my own, because Jesus was there with me. And I experienced yet more of the upholding power of praise through that time - which has never left me.

Once again I was living on my own - this time after sharing for nearly 25 years, and there was certainly some adjusting to do! And once again I was taken into a deeper place of living on my own, but knowing that Jesus was always with me. It was also again a time when Father taught me more about taking one day at a time - knowing that He would show me what I should be doing each day; and not worrying or getting anxious about the days that lay ahead. I'm not saying I mastered it all in one go and there wasn't any heartache along the way; but the Holy Spirit helped me step by step going forward and strengthened me and loved me through it.

What Now?

A friend emailed me and shared how, although the 'normality' of my life with Maureen had gone completely, in due course the Lord would take me into new 'normal' life that He had planned for me. This really resonated in my spirit and I was very grateful to the Lord, and to my friend, for pointing this out. I was moving into a new season and He would show me and be with me every step of the way.

Do you remember me sharing how the Lord took us on occasion to a small group in Bridgwater that met on a Sunday evening? Well a friend from there invited me to go along there that first Sunday of being on my own. I really felt I needed some 'input' and was grateful to the Lord for the invitation.

During the days following, the Lord reminded me of the DVD's I had from the High Leigh conferences; and also the music cd's, and even some cassette tapes from the time before cd's! I started watching the DVD's, probably for about roughly 15 mins, before I went to bed. This was so encouraging as the Lord used them to feed me and build up His strength in me to cope with all that was going on.

And the music cd's? Well we usually got two copies each year, as we played them so much we weren't sure whether we'd wear them out.... So I was able to have copies in the house and in the car. Again, as with the DVD's, the Lord showed me a 'strategy' and in the morning I'd set one playing before I left to go up the garden to open up the chickens so..... as I came back into the house afterwards they were playing and it didn't feel as though I was coming into an empty house! In the car they came on as I turned the engine on and I can't begin to tell you how many times the song that came on would be exactly what I needed to lift me and take me on to the next step of my journey that day.... And that is still the case right up until the present time.

Nights weren't always easy, although I tended to get off to sleep reasonably well - mainly because I was so tired. I don't think I had realised just how tired I was after the months of Maureen being ill and looking after her, etc. I was so pleased to have been able to and that she was able to stay at home right through to the end. Anyway - back to the 'nights'.... I had a tendency to wake up in the early hours and it was then, very often, that the enemy used to try and have a go at me and especially tried to make me fearful. But God!! It was those nights when the Lord first started giving me what I've since called, 'night songs' - a good majority of them being the songs that I'd learned back in the 70's and 80's and a lot of them scripture songs.

One night stands out and, I suppose was a sort of turning point, as I don't think I actually slept that night! For a start I couldn't get off to sleep, which was unusual, and the enemy right from early on was trying to run me around in my thoughts, and I started fighting off the thoughts with songs. I don't think I was necessarily singing them out loud all the time but they were definitely singing in my head! And basically I just carried on all night and, amazingly, when I got up next morning I didn't feel as though I'd been awake all night! I'd certainly learned another very practical lesson, in a very real way - that I could hold off the enemy's attacks with praise and worship!

I've shared these few paragraphs under the heading "What Now?" because I wanted you to see how the Lord prepared me step by step for the new season He was taking me into - which He alone knew, because He had planned it all....

Always remember that nothing that happens in our lives is a surprise to the Lord - because He's planned it. And everything that happens, as He takes us into a new season, we can be in peace about - because He has planned it.

CHAPTER 8

My Onward Journey with Jesus

8/1 TBC – New Vision, New Challenges

What Next?

Towards the end of the October of 2014 I went along to a new church that had started in Bridgwater around the end of the previous year, but I was not aware of it until the Easter of that year - just when Maureen became ill. A friend had started going there and I felt I should go and visit! I felt a bit nervous that first Sunday morning when I went to my first meeting at what was known then as the SOZO church (Saved, Healed and Delivered).... this was the start of the church that eventually became The Blessing Church (TBC).

As well as my friend already there and going on a regular basis, when I went that first morning, I found there were several other people there that I knew. The room was set up in what I call the standard, rather conventional way - several rows of chairs with a gap between, so there were basically two blocks..... all facing the front. They were in a slight curve rather than a completely straight line. After my years at Kingston Fellowship, where we had the chairs in a rectangular formation with all of us facing one another, I still found it a bit strange being in rows facing the front!

However, over the years I'd got used to whatever layout the chairs were placed in - what was important was what happened in the meeting.... I felt that the Lord's presence was there and when Pastor Joe Benjamin began to minister the Word I knew, without a shadow of a doubt, from the response in my spirit, that I was in the right place and this was where the Lord wanted me to be!

The most important part of where we fellowship in the Body - is that we are where God wants us to be and where He wants to use us to build His Kingdom. If you really want to know this, the Lord will show you - although, more than likely in different ways for different people. It was the response in my spirit that confirmed it for me - but, as I said, the Lord shows us and confirms things in different ways.

A New Fellowship - A New Life

After that weekend in the October, when I first attended the new church in Bridgwater, I continued to go there.... and the rest, as they say, is 'history'! I believed that was where the Lord wanted me to be in the Body at that time! Hallelujah!

Having read Chapter 7/2 you might remember that I was a bit out of practice in attending on a weekly basis for any length of time, but am glad to say I had no problem getting back to it! Actually I enjoyed the regularity of once again meeting weekly and getting to know the other people who attended the church. And that's what I felt I should concentrate on initially - getting to know people and learning more about their journey and relationship with the Lord. And helping, where the opportunity arose, with whatever was needed. We usually had 'tea and cake' (or coffee!) after the meeting, so help was usually needed in the kitchen - and most people open up more when chatting over the washing up!

Do you remember what I said towards the end of the last chapter that, after Maureen had gone to be with Lord, a friend emailed me? She shared how, although the 'normality' of my life with Maureen had gone completely, in due course the Lord would take me into a new 'normal' life that He had planned for me.

Gradually, I began to realise that this was now beginning to happen as I became more involved in the new fellowship that I was becoming part of and moved into a new, and quite different season of my life.

It didn't happen overnight, and I don't think anyone would expect it to - especially not after having spent nearly 25 years sharing your life with someone. But whatever happens in our lives to bring about a change of circumstance - it's important to continue to go forward and into what Father has planned for you in the next season.

Early Days of the Church

Pastors Joe and Josie Benjamin who had come to this country from Zimbabwe, moved from Wimbledon, South London to Bridgwater in Somerset in August of 2013. Prior to Wimbledon they were based in the Sheffield area, but had moved to Wimbledon in January 2011 for Joe to be able to take part in more dentistry training, his profession at that time. A month after arriving in Wimbledon their first child, Jael a girl, was born; and their second child, Jair a boy, was born in January 2013.

Their reason for arriving in Bridgwater in August 2013 was to start a church! It was a place they had never heard of before, so why Bridgwater? They simply believed that the Lord had told them to go - and their desire was, and still is, to be obedient to whatever He asks them to do!

They hired a place known as Blue Doors to start meetings in Bridgwater, and to begin with there was only Joe, Josie and their two small children - and gradually the Lord began to add to their number! This was all before my time - but I've heard Joe share as to what happened. By the time I started in the October of 2014 I believe there were around 40 to 50 in the fellowship.

There was freedom in the meetings, and what I mean by that is - the Holy Spirit was allowed to move freely through those who were prepared to let Him use them. I found it a privilege, as the Lord began to help me to become a part of this new church fellowship, to be there and to be part of what He was doing.

I firmly believe, without any doubt, that there are simply no coincidences with God - and I would imagine that you'll have

probably realised that by now! I also believe that the people we are in contact with, whether it be at work, at church, or anywhere in between; are the ones that He wants us to have contact with. So really, unless the Holy Spirit shows us otherwise, those we are in contact with are basically 'God contacts' - even if we initially might wish they weren't! That's when we need to change our 'Mind Set' and ask Father why He's got us in contact with them...... and what He wants us to do as part of His plan!

Becoming Part of a New Church Family

So.... what was the Lord doing with this new, young church fellowship - made up of a variety of people, all with different church back grounds? And what was I doing in the middle of it all? I could probably answer that now - but I need really to share with you how the Lord was developing this young church - and developing me and my role in it at the same time, as well as preparing me for what He had on His heart for me in the future.

I began to get to know Joe and Josie better and started to realise that currently, possibly because of it being the early days of the church, that the responsibility of most of what was happening was on their shoulders..... There was an older man who took responsibility for sorting out the arrangement of the room before and after the meeting - but it was usually Joe who was helping him! On arrival the room would have rows of tables with chairs - and these all had to be moved out of the way. The tables were mostly stacked out of the way, some of the chairs put out for the meeting and the rest stacked with the tables. And then afterwards everything had to be put back once the meeting was over!

The organisation of the kitchen and setting up the 'cakes and drinks', etc - seemed to be left to Josie, although more helpers, for washing up etc afterwards, were beginning to come forward and pitch in.

The other big part of the Sunday morning jigsaw, was the setting up of all the equipment for the Worship Team (after the room set up was completed) - mainly managed by the team but with Joe involved and helping with that as well. The keyboard was played by Nick, who brought his own keyboard with him - so there was just the sound equipment needed there.... But this was transported by Joe (it was stored at his home) each week in a small van - which needed unloading and reloading before and after each meeting..... Plus the setting up of the screen which had the words of the songs put on it via the computer, with the necessary software. Bob was in charge of this when I first started going, and then a young man, by the name of James, took it on.

Please believe me, when I say I'm not sharing this to be critical - I believe the Lord was highlighting the situation to me, because He wanted me to do something about it! You might remember I said earlier that, in the early days / weeks of being at the church, I felt I should concentrate on getting to know people and give help in any way I was able to!

As well as meeting on a Sunday morning, those who wanted and were able to, met together for prayer on a Tuesday evening - known as 'Hour of Power'! We met at the house of an older lady called Betty, known generally in the fellowship as 'Mother Betty' - and around a dozen of us gathered there each week. Usually Bob and Phil, a couple of men from a church in Burnham, also joined us. Joe had helped and guided Bob into moving into a healing ministry and he felt the continuing contact was a help to him, and Phil loved to come as he also knew Betty. Joe usually came on a Tuesday and also brought his guitar with him for worship.

Initially there were only a few children with us on a Sunday morning, but as more joined us something was needed specifically for them during the time that the Word was being ministered. The person who was already spending some time with them, asked me if I'd be willing to help - and somehow I found myself heading up what, eventually became a small Sunday School! There were 4 of us and I organised a rota, with 2 of us on each week - giving the remaining 2 the opportunity to be in the meeting. It didn't happen overnight, but think it was probably in place by the end of 2014.

This was very much a 'new beginning' (season) for me - a time to listen, observe, be sensitive to what was happening and, most importantly, listen carefully to what Father was saying to me in it all.... It certainly wasn't a time to 'rush in and take over' in any way - and I had no desire to. I'm so thankful to the Lord for taking me forward a step at a time at His pace. Apart from offering to help in the kitchen when needed - I realise, looking back now, that the other things I got involved in were as a result of being asked to do so! I would encourage those of you going into new situations to be open to the Lord to show you what He wants of you in them. Don't 'rush in' but move step by step in His timing - you, and He, will accomplish so much more.....

More Changes and New Challenges

At some stage in the summer of 2015, possibly towards the end of it, I found my self joining the Worship Team..... I believe we'd had an 'Open Mic Sunday', when Joe would encourage as many of us as possible to share something. He said: "Whatever hidden talents you have, come and bless the church."

It had been a long time since I'd played my guitar and sung, and especially not in public; so you can imagine the shock, when I realised the Lord was saying that I should play and sing something on the 'Open Mic Sunday'! I shared a couple of the songs that the Lord had used to help me after He had taken Maureen home, and testified a little of what I'd been learning about the power of praise at that time. I think it was after that I somehow found myself included in the Worship Team. I'd always loved to sing and worship the Lord and I found it a great privilege to be part of the team.

I believe it was probably around that time that Joe also spoke to me about becoming a trustee of the church. Joe had gone through all the necessary paperwork that was needed in order to register the church as a charity, and on 8 July 2015 we became the Eagle Mountain Church Charity and, after that the church itself was also called 'Eagle Mountain'. He asked me to talk to the Lord about being the fourth trustee - he, Josie, and another member of the church, Esther, were the other three trustees.

This was definitely another 'first' for me - but, when I asked the Lord about it, I felt He wanted me to go ahead. Only Father knew what that was going to eventually involve and the challenges

I would face through it and, to be honest, I'm glad I didn't know.... but I'm 'jumping the gun' a bit there!

Through the years I have found that it's through the challenges that I face, that I grow the most in my walk and relationship with the Lord. I'm not saying it's easy and some of them, as you've heard, are the opposite of being easy but I do know I grow! And you will too, if you face the challenges in your life and ask the Holy Spirit to go through them with you and to help you.

A Slightly Different Sort of Challenge

When I first started attending the church I found that the Lord always had so much to say to me through Joe's ministry - I felt I should make notes, so I could go back over them in the week! One week, in the summer of 2015 I believe, Joe said in advance that he would be speaking about 'depression' on the following Sunday. Carol, my friend who had originally told me about the church, was going to be away and asked if I could let her have a copy of the notes as she wanted to share them with a friend.....

I put the notes together but felt I'd like Joe to check it through before giving them to Carol - so took them with me on the Tuesday evening prayer time at Betty's. I showed them to him afterwards, before he went off home in his car, and we ended up having quite a long talk. He said they were fine and in line with what he shared. Somehow we got onto the fact that I used to teach business studies and that, when I was self-employed, I used to do proof reading.

Our conversation resulted in Joe asking me about the possibility of my proof reading his current book that he was writing - "A Lifestyle of Prayer"..... Wow! I wasn't expecting that, but I felt it was such a privilege to have been asked - and I certainly said "Yes!" And basically, I've been 'proof reading' his books, and anything else that's needed to be, ever since!

I sometimes marvel at how the Lord fits 'all the pieces' in our lives together to produce what He has planned. It's only as I've been 'writing' this book that I've come anywhere near to understanding some of what He's done through the years. I've said how the 'proof reading' etc was a different sort of challenge - mainly because of the part it played in 'unrolling' a whole myriad of other things, many of them challenges in themselves. I will share more with you in the next section of this chapter.....

8/2 Growth, More Training and Change

God 'Unrolls' More Changes

The paperwork, etc involved in me becoming the fourth trustee of Eagle Mountain was eventually completed - though it took a while, as these things often do.... Once everything was completed and officially in order - we set up our first official Trustees Meeting in the January of 2016. As trustees we had to meet officially at least four times a year - with recorded minutes that could be kept on file and produced if the Charity Commission requested them. I don't suppose it takes much guessing on your part, to realise who would be taking the minutes!

One of the first things we needed to sort when we first met, was the issue of getting an accountant. As a registered charity we had to produce accredited accounts, needing to be done by a professional accountant - with the 'knock on' affect of needing a proper set of accounts to be accredited! Again - not much guessing to know where we were heading with that side of the equation.....

Joe took on the task of finding an accountant and was helped through a contact at one of the other churches in town. I took on the setting up of a proper set of accounts, comprising the two bank accounts we had. Our new accountant was a great help as he created a basic spread sheet, which I was able to adapt to what we needed for our church.

It was getting on for about 30 years since I'd done anything with spread sheets - although 'back in the day' I did use to teach one day intensive courses on them for Adult Education. I went through tutorial courses on the internet to refresh my memory - and trusted the rest to the Lord to help me.... It's such an education to have the Holy Spirit teach you what you need to know!! On the practical side concerning the 'physical' money that was given to the church on a Sunday morning - Esther (also a trustee) and myself counted and recorded it together at the end of the meeting. Then I would pay it into the bank in the week and, of course, record it on the spread sheets.

Along with the Annual Accounts we would also have to produce an Annual Report on the Charity which would have to be posted, alongside the Annual Accounts, on the Charity Commission's website every year.. I have to confess to finding the Report side of things far more daunting than the accounts! But God is always so faithful - He again took me step by step through it all, showing me how to do things I really didn't have a clue about. This was particularly true when it came to uploading everything on to the government website. I did it several times in the years before we closed the Charity - but I didn't know how to do it then.... and I still don't – it was entirely the Lord's grace enabling me!

As I entered into the new year of 2016, I began to realise that the Lord had taken me into a new season of growth and training - I was definitely learning new and challenging things, and growing in the process! And, as I look back now, I am even more aware that He took me and taught me the things I needed to go

forward in all He had planned for me.

I would encourage you again, not to discount any of the things that happen in your life. Believe me when I say that nothing in your life is ever wasted - God will always use it for your benefit, or someone else's.... or both!

More Organization

In those first few months of 2016, as well as the setting up of the framework of the Charity we had become, Joe also introduced us to Coordinator Teams. He asked various members to head up the lead on each of the teams covering the main areas of the life of the church, and then recruit other members to join the team to help with the task in hand. These covered worship, prayer, children, and so on and, because we still weren't that many in number, some of us were in more than one team....

We had regular Coordinator meetings with the leaders of the different teams and Joe shared what was on his heart in regard to the working of each of them. And the leaders of each of the teams were encouraged to meet and have their own meetings. By then I was taking minutes for all the meetings taking place. I think it was around that time possibly, that Joe started calling me his 'PA'.....!

That time in the first few months of 2016 was very much a time of refreshing skills I had learned previously and learning a whole load of new ones.... very much a challenging time! Joe would often 'run' ideas past me - and then leave them with me to be put into practice with the help of the Holy Spirit, and organise what was needed. One of his many gifts is to see the

potential in people and, guided by the Holy Spirit, draw that potential out of them. I'm aware that I wouldn't be in the place I am now if the Lord hadn't used him to do that, and am so thankful to Father, and to Joe, for helping me in this way. And to Josie for working with Joe, because obviously she is very much part of the partnership in it all. I will share more in this area as we go forward.

On the Move

Yes, those first few months of 2016 were definitely busy ones! You see, we were also looking for another venue to hold our Sunday morning meetings in.... The place where we met - called the Blue Doors, was called that because literally, the entrance doors were painted blue and made it easy for people to find. The building was owned by the local Masonic Lodge and, unfortunately, we had heard that some people hadn't wanted to visit us because of it. We took it as a triumph of the Lord that His name was being lifted high in the enemy's territory - but understood people might have reservations!

At the first of our trustee meetings we had discussed buildings and, in particular, the position reached of a new, large community hall being built at Wembdon Green, an area of Bridgwater. It was agreed that we would try and secure temporary accommodation, until such time as it became available.

Out of the four of us trustees, both Joe and Esther worked full time and Josie's time was pretty hectic looking after Joe and the children, etc - so it seemed sensible for it to be me who went 'hunting'! If the others heard of any possibilities, they let me know of them to follow up.... and some of them, available to view at the weekend, we were able to go and look at together.

We eventually tracked down a Recreation Centre on an area of Bridgwater called Hamp, which was run by the YMCA. To be honest it felt a bit 'shabby' initially but we were able to do a 'paint job' on the meeting room - which vastly improved it! It had a small room at the back which we were able to use for Sunday School and a kitchen area with space around it to have 'tea and cake'..... It also had a tarmac area outside - suitable for youngsters and bbq's in the better weather! We moved into that venue in the May of 2016 and were there for just under 18 months.

Moving forward in what you believe the Lord wants you to do isn't always straight forward, and very often doesn't always happen very quickly. The enemy will do his utmost to disrupt the process and we need to be aware of that and listen to the leading of the Holy Spirit in it all. With His help we need to learn to discern what Father is saying in the situation, and what is the disruptive work of the enemy that we have to rise above.... And this was our experience in our search for a new venue. It took time and energy and, most of all, persistence to accomplish what we believed the Lord had shown us to do.

I would encourage you to be persistent in following what Father has put on your heart to do - and don't give up as the enemy brings the challenges. But do be alert and sensitive in doing what the Holy Spirit shows you!

Book Challenge

It was also at the beginning of May in 2016, that the subject of me writing a book popped its head up again.... If you remember, I shared earlier in my story about how I thought the Lord had spoken to me about it in the early eighties - when I was living in Surbiton over 30 years before! At the time I never took it forward any further – I didn't think it was something I was capable of and never really asked the Lord for His help to do it.

Fast forward to the evening of 3 May 2016 (I noted the date because it made such an impression on me), I was already in bed and was listening to Joe broadcasting on Periscope. He had not long started broadcasting on a regular basis and I tried to join him when he did. You can possibly imagine how amazed I was when I heard him say that: "....there are books in some of those of you watching this, and there are people waiting to read those books, so they can be helped and encouraged."

I have to say it felt as though he knew my situation and was speaking directly to me, although I knew he didn't know anything about the time the Lord had spoken to me about writing a book back in the eighties. But of course I knew that the Lord had spoken to me then, and that now He had spoken to me again - and that this time I couldn't ignore it....

I didn't ignore it - but at the same time I didn't do a great deal about it! And I certainly didn't say anything to anyone - not even to Joe to acknowledge how the Lord had spoken to me through what he said. What I did do, straight after I'd been challenged, was to make a note (as I said above) of the date and circumstances and then write down a few notes - a sort of 'introduction' that it might be possible to include in the future when I came to write the book. Yes, I'd taken on board that at some stage there would be a book but knew somehow it would be later on - currently the Lord had me too involved with all that was happening in the present!

Some of what I wrote down that night was as follows:

"So, why do I think I am qualified to write a book? I don't think that I am qualified, in fact it is just the opposite! BUT God is able and with Him all things are possible and I am still learning that I need to move out into the unknown and follow where He leads me - even if it scares me, and I end up 'doing it afraid' as Joyce Meyer (a well known minister of the Word) often shares." hopefully it gives you some idea of what I was feeling.....

This is something I'll be coming back to at a later stage....

Once again I'm marvelling at God's timing and realising how little I really understand it! As I write this I realise that, when He first spoke to me back in the early eighties about writing a book and sharing how He turned the tide in my life - what He was doing was planting a seed. He knew even then, exactly what He was going to do with that seed - even though I certainly didn't.....

There are some seeds of plants that fall to the ground and are buried that don't actually grow into anything until literally years later. That first 'book seed' was one of those! It was 30 years before any movement started in that seed on that night in early May 2016, when the Lord challenged me through what Joe was

sharing.... with very little growth following for several more years! I hope to share with you how He eventually brought about the growth needed, to the point of it flourishing as it is currently.... In the writing of this book.

On the Move Again

As I explained earlier, we knew our time at the Recreation Centre would be temporary and, as we approached the autumn of 2017 it looked as though we would be on the move again! The hall at Wembdon Green was starting to function in 2017. Joe began to make contact with the managing committee concerning us meeting there on a Sunday morning and, after a fair amount of negotiation, we were able to start meeting there by the October. Part of the 'negotiation' was that as part of our service to the community we committed to cleaning up from events held on the previous Saturday evening, before we set up our equipment etc. This was mainly because of the difficulty of getting early morning cleaners prior to us needing to be there.... It worked!

Joe had it firmly in his spirit that this was where we should be meeting - and didn't give up when difficulties rose up! As I said earlier in this chapter - if we have been given something by the Lord, then we need to be persistent in pursuing it and seeing it through.... Even, and especially, when we're faced with challenges in doing so. In this instance our biggest challenge was our commitment to clean the hall before we used it on a Sunday morning - but I believe this was such a witness to the Management Committee of God's grace in action. And out of it came a firm friendship with the person who was managing it,

which has persisted through the years since! Don't let the lies of the enemy move you off course, but keep persisting in all Father has shown you to do.

The Bigger Vision

Joe and Josie had always been open about the fact that their vision from the Lord was always greater than it being confined to Bridgwater. Sadly, looking back, I don't think the church as a whole understood this and seemed unable to take it 'on board'.... In fact, other than Esther and myself, I don't believe anyone else really 'caught' it.

Joe had never seen himself as a 'stay at home' pastor, but much more a church 'planter' - and then moving on to where the Lord led him, to plant more churches elsewhere. At the end of November 2017 the 'Benjamin' family moved up to the Birmingham area, which is where Joe felt the Lord wanted them to be for their next step forward - and moved into a house in Wolverhampton.

As trustees of the Eagle Mountain church in Bridgwater, we had envisaged the Lord raising someone of His choice who would pastor the church, guided and helped by Joe - as he moved up to another area. In the absence of that having happened - Joe, and when possible Josie and the children with him, came down on a Sunday to lead the meeting and minister to those still attending the church. This was a tremendous commitment on his and the family's part as he worked full time and it was quite a drive down and back every week!

By this time we had also become known as The Blessing Church, but still within the Eagle Mountain Charity. This had resulted from all the Lord had been saying, and highlighting to Joe, concerning The Blessing - starting with His blessing of Adam and continuing down through his lineage - right through to us today. This isn't the place to share more on this, but I would point you to: www.theblessingmovement.org where you can find much more about The Blessing Movement which it has now become!

I will share with you that the initial broadcasting online by Joe in 2016 (which is how Father spoke to me the second time about this book) has now grown into a large and very active online ministry. This was increased, as you can probably imagine, through the circumstances of the pandemic which we have been through with the inability to meet through all the various lockdowns..... Once more I marvel at God's timing!

I think it wise for us to realise that we probably never have the whole vision of what the Lord is doing in our lives, or a complete picture of what He is doing on a wider scale. In our situation at TBC - if you're asking the question as to why the Lord didn't raise up someone to lead the church when He moved Joe and the family up to the midlands..... I can't give you an answer, because I don't know.

I can think of one or two situations in my own experience through the years, when I've been ready to move forward on something, but the other person(s) haven't - what I was believing would happen, didn't. At the end of the day, the Lord always gives us the choice to say yes or no - and not everybody chooses to say 'yes'.....

The Tide is Flowing

Looking back through the years I realise there have been seasons when the tide, since it 'turned' in my life at the beginning of the '70's', has definitely flowed at quite a pace. In the early part of 2018 there was the beginning of another 'flow', which was only possible because it followed a previous one which happened when I became part of TBC (The Blessing Church) in Bridgwater. I could share other instances, but I'll just stick with sharing this latest 'flow' - starting, as I said, in early 2018, and still flowing ever more strongly and influencing how I come to be writing this book that you are reading....

It was in January 2018 that we began making 'Declarations' every Sunday morning in the TBC meeting. Let me explain more fully! I'm sure you'll understand when I speak of the power there is in God's Word and how, when we speak out the truths it contains, it is released into our lives. I believe this is particularly true when we speak these truths out in the form of declarations of what the Word says. The Lord put this on Joe's heart and, from the New Year onwards we stood, as a body of believers in unity, and declared aloud together 7 Declarations, based on specific verses in the Word and put together by Joe - one for each day of the week.

They became very much a part of our time and celebration together. People were so blessed that soon they were being printed out so we could all take home a copy with us for the week for our encouragement! One of the coordinator groups was an Intercessors Prayer group with a group on WhatsApp where we could post prayer requests for all those in the group to be able to join in prayer. Three of us soon began to split the 7 days between us and post the declarations for those days in the group and adding any thoughts that the Lord gave us to share.

Over a period of time it changed to two of us, and eventually I took over posting for the whole week - a blessing and a challenge, wrapped up in one! I expanded it slightly with a sentence or two explaining a little about the verse the declaration was based on. I've shared more on how I did this, plus an example, further on. The number of recipients of the declarations also grew! By then we had groups on WhatsApp for TBC Tribe as well as quite a number of individual people who received them, as well as The Blessing Tribe and The Blessing Church pages on FaceBook.

It wasn't too long before people began to think that they would like to be able to have them in print in some sort of book form, to enable them to be seen, other than just in a 'post' online. That is how The Blessing Daily began to take shape..... which I will share more of in due course!

I learned so much as I began the task of posting the declarations on a daily basis - and have to say that I still do, as I continue to post them! I believe they played a large part in 'training' me in 'writing' - something I had never been very skilful in.... I don't think I'd be writing this book currently, if Father hadn't trained and prepared me to do so. One of the ways He prepared the way, was through getting me involved in the declarations.

The Declarations

I'd like to share a little more with you about the Declarations, and give you a more comprehensive view of what they actually are - and what is posted on a daily basis....

First of all - this is an example of a 'set' of declarations produced each week:

THE BLESSING WEEKLY DECLARATIONS

1. I will forgive anyone that has wronged me and I will love them with the Love of God. (Colossians 3:13)
2. I will be a shining light to everyone in my sphere of influence. (Matthew 5:14-16)
3. Oh Holy Spirit open my spiritual eyes to see you more clearly. (Ephesians 1:18)
4. Any barriers to my promotion are broken. I receive spiritual and physical promotion in the Name of Jesus. (Psalm 75:6-7)
5. Fear is defeated and has been replaced by ferocious faith in my life. (Isaiah 43:1)
6. My life shall be a living testimony of God's favour and grace far and wide. (2 Timothy 1:8)
7. The church of Jesus Christ is moving on, the devil lost his power on the Cross and we walk triumphantly. (Philippians 3:12-14)

I DECLARE THAT THE BLESSING
IS WORKING IN MY LIFE!"

This is from the end of September 2019 and, back then, as a church, we would have stood and declared these together on the Sunday morning. Nowadays I send them out on a Sunday morning, along with the first declaration of the week.

From this set that I've shared with you - this is what I posted on the Sunday:

> "We are commanded by Paul to.....
>
> "Tolerate the weaknesses of those in the family of faith, forgiving one another in the same way you have been graciously forgiven by Jesus Christ. If you find fault with someone, release this same gift of forgiveness to them." Colossians 3:13 TPT
>
> ....he also says we need to be "....patient with each other, making allowance for each other's faults..." Why? Because of our love for each other! (Ephesians 4:2)
>
> And Jesus Himself tells us that....
>
> ".....when you are praying, first forgive anyone you are holding a grudge against, so that your Father in heaven will forgive your sins, too. ". Mark 11:25 NLT
>
> Let's Determine in our hearts today to Declare that, with Father's help and His Grace....
>
> "I will forgive anyone that has wronged me and I will love them with the Love of God."

These have become a powerful 'tool' and, yes, a 'weapon' in my own life and walk with Jesus. The enemy doesn't like it when we combat his lies with the Word of God - which is exactly what Jesus did when they met 'head to head' in the 40 days He spent in the wilderness, before He started out in His ministry. And, even more so, he hates it when we make a personalised declaration based on a specific Word, which makes a statement in our lives and opens up the way for the power of the Holy Spirit to work to bring it to pass!

I can't begin to share with you the number of times that Father has given me the answer I've needed via a specific declaration. Nor the way He challenges me through them over something happening in my life. And, when the enemy is trying to 'run me around' on anything, especially in the night, instead of arguing - I head for the declarations and continue in the preparation of them or the 'daily'. And again, so often I find myself comforted and strengthened with just the word I need in that moment.

I would encourage you, if you don't already, to start including the declaration of the Word in your walk with Jesus. There are many sources to find help with them. Or, better still, create your own! Even take a verse that Father shows you and speak it out in the 'first person' so it refers to you personally.

I believe you will find it to be such a help - especially when facing any particular difficulty.

8/3 A Completely New Season Arrives

Change On the Way

As autumn moved into winter in 2018 Joe began talks with David Parker, the lead Pastor at Riverside Church in Taunton. This was after he'd shown an interest in what was happening at TBC and a possible church plant in Bridgwater by Riverside.

Before I share more about that I need to explain that, through the year numbers had dwindled and, by this time we were down to a handful of regulars.... Add to that, the toll on Joe of commuting every Sunday down to Bridgwater - and I think we all realised that something needed to change!

It was agreed that there would be a three month trial period, January to March of 2019, with Riverside sending over a worship leader plus speaker for three out of the four Sundays with Dave also taking a turn in coming to preach. The other Sunday Bob (who used to come down from Burnham to pray with us on a Tuesday evening) would come and preach and we would provide our own worship.... During that time Esther and myself met with Dave and his wife Karen to look at all that would be involved, etc.

At the end of April The Blessing Church in Bridgwater came to an end; and a branch of Riverside Church in Bridgwater began. One of my main tasks at that time was to close the Eagle Mountain Charity - another challenge - and investigations began by Riverside regarding setting up another charity for their new church plant.

You would probably realise that, in many ways, this was a difficult time with all that was happening. The basic running of the church was mainly still in the hands of Esther and myself, with the responsibilities of the building, etc still with TBC. This was changed over to Riverside at the start of May, although the 'on the ground' responsibilities continued to remain with us.

Esther and myself continued there for a good part of 2019 as we felt it right to do all we could to assist the change over. We both moved on, early in the October. We both felt at that point, that we needed to be 'out of the equation' to leave the new 'plant' to move forward, feeling that as long as we were still there TBC Bridgwater was still very much part of what was happening.

It was very much a time of change and the ending of one season - the beginning of another! But, at the risk of repeating myself, these are times when we learn so much - as long as we are willing to move with the Lord and be open to learn from them. So often they are challenging, because we are 'comfortable' where we are and changes always 'rock the boat'. God is in the business of building His Kingdom and growth can't happen without movement forward!

Our part is to be willing, to be obedient and to act on what He shows us. And we definitely need to focus on going forward into all He has prepared for us - and not be looking back at the past and dwelling on it. I've often heard Joyce Meyer say "where our thoughts are - we will follow"! I want to go forward into all Father has - not to dwell on the past and live there!

A New, But Not So New Fellowship

Can I take you back to the second section of Chapter 7 - where I shared with you the move Maureen and I made to Bridgwater in May 1991? Do you remember me sharing how we joined the Bridgwater Community Church and were there until we moved out to Watchet in West Somerset in January '93? You've probably guessed by now, as to where the Lord took me after my time at TBC.... "Yes" that's right - back to BCC!

Well before all the changes started taking place at TBC - I had become involved as a volunteer with a charity working in Bridgwater called Grace Advocacy, and a team made up of people from some of the different churches in the town. It helps people who had got into debt, alongside giving help in applying for various benefits - including disability benefits such as PIP (Personal Independent Payment) and AA (Attendance Allowance) and acting as advocates for them in their difficult situations.

At that point, about 4 to 5 years ago, there were two teams - one in the Richmond/Kingston area, where Gary Holland who set up the charity was based; and one here in Bridgwater. Now there are several over in the east of England and, locally, there's another one up in Burnham, just up the coast from Bridgwater. The leader of our local team is Alan Cable - part of BCC and the main base for Grace Advocacy in town where we held lunches to encourage our clients, prior to the onset of the pandemic.

I went with my sister and niece to visit my other sister and brother in Australia in the October/November of 2019 and, on my return, took a few weeks off! And then at the start of 2020, nearly thirty years after Maureen and I first went there, I started back at BCC.... There were several folk there from when I was there the first time round, plus Alan and his wife - so some familiar faces. We'd had contact off and on through the years and, more recently, I had seen Colin (main leader) at the local Church Forum which meets every quarter. I was there as representative of TBC as Joe was unable to attend as he worked full time.

I do love the way Father 'knits' everything together in our lives, and this is another example when He took me back to BCC after so many years - right to where Maureen and I had first started in fellowship in Bridgwater..... I was made very welcome and I appreciated being back in this part of the body - with the added association with Grace Advocacy.

The Blessing Movement

Alongside what was happening at TBC Bridgwater - in Birmingham Joe was making steps towards planting TBC Birmingham and, in March 2019, a small group started to meet there on a Sunday evening. As I've shared - The Blessing Church in Bridgwater came to an end at the end of April 2019; but TBC in Birmingham continued through that year and into the next.... until the pandemic struck. But, although there are currently no meetings 'on the ground' - The Blessing Movement continues online; and it's a privilege to be part of what the Lord continues to do. And, as I shared towards the end of the last section of this chapter, it has grown into a large and very active online ministry.

I continue to work with Joe in whatever way I can be of help, although my main task these days is looking after the declarations

- which I put together as the Holy Spirit leads me. We send out a prophetic word once a week to all those receiving the declarations - both in text and audio format. Joe sends me the prophetic words and I proof read them for him and send back a copy.....

I count it a privilege to have been part of the Blessing Movement right through from the early days, and continue to do so. I am aware of learning a great deal through the years from working with Joe and Josie and their family, and so appreciate their love and what the Lord has done in me through their love, encouragement and fellowship. Needless to say - I'm still learning - and expect to continue to do so until Father takes me home!

The Blessing Daily

I mentioned earlier that there was interest in some of those receiving the declarations, concerning having them put together in print in some form of book so it was possible to go back to at other times. Joe and I both felt a stirring in our spirits over this, feeling the Lord wanted us to move forward on the suggestion. I think we realised that in print something more substantial was needed than what I was posting on a daily basis online. We both prayed and I began to put an outline plan together for a daily reading.

Initially we were aiming for a devotional with 'dates', but not confined to a specific year. However, more recently we felt we should move towards producing something that's suitable for daily study, but no dates just a heading, which they were in fact already being given. This will make it less restrictive, with readers just being able to 'dip in' for encouragement at any time they need to.

Again, initially the plan was for me to put the outline pages together, plus a few possible thoughts and then send a week of the daily to Joe to expand the content with what the Lord gave him. I prepared the first week and found myself putting more than just a few thoughts down - anyway, I sent him the first week for him to work on.... Next thing - Joe rang me and gave me rather a shock. He explained that, as he was going through to see what the Lord wanted him to do with it - He stopped him! He believed that the Lord said it was to stay as it was and he could leave it all with me for the Holy Spirit to guide me in the content of it all. And that's how we've continued - I put it together with Father's guidance, and then send it a week at a time to Joe to look through. I feel happier if he checks it through - I'd hate it to have anything that wasn't in line with scripture! Oh, and our vision is for more than one volume to be produced.....!

I will share with you a little further on about how I go about putting the 'daily' together....

God is so good! I am fully aware that none of the above would have been, or is possible without the Holy Spirit guiding and showing me what to do - both directly and through others, especially through working with Joe and Josie. There are some occasions that, in the midst of preparing a new page for the daily and putting the 'content' section together - I suddenly realise that the verse, the declaration and, particularly, what I've written in the content section - is just exactly spot on for the challenge being faced by myself on that specific day - and it so amazes me. I know

it's God's grace and love poured out on me in abundance and I'm so thankful to Him.

A 'Taste' of the Daily

At the end of Chapter 8/2 I gave you an example set of declarations that I shared with you, plus an example of the first post (the Sunday) of that particular set. I'd now like share with you how the verse and the declaration from that first post, has been used as a basis for a page in The Blessing Daily - so you can understand the process.....

"I Will Forgive"

Colossians 3:13 NLT "Make allowance for each other's faults, and forgive anyone who offends you. Remember, the Lord forgave you, so you must forgive others."

Saying we'll forgive someone is very easy to say, and very difficult to actually do - at least it is for me; and without God's grace I think it's impossible!

But Mark tells us very clearly in relation to us praying to ".....remember that it's not all asking. If you have anything against someone, forgive..." (Mark 11:25 MSG) and that it's only then that we can be forgiven. I'm sure we're all aware of saying in the Lord's Prayer - "forgive us our sins, as we forgive others". And in our Declaration verse today - "Forgive as quickly and completely as the Master forgave you." (Colossians 3:13 MSG)

But WHY? Why is it so important that we forgive those who've hurt us and treated us wrongly, etc.... too many things to be able to begin to list them all here.....
We forgive completely and only based on Jesus love and forgiveness toward us - not on anything that anyone else has done. When I forgive someone I set a prisoner free... and that prisoner is me! Without forgiveness in my life, I lay myself open to endlessly being run around by resentment and retaliation, that will also be further stoked by the lies of the enemy.
The only way that I will live in peace and grow in my walk with Jesus; and have an open path in prayer to my Father - is to "*forgive*".
BLESSING DECLARATION "I will forgive anyone that has wronged me and I will love them with the Love of God."

FURTHER STUDY. Mark 11:25, Ephesians 4:2

Now, let me tell you more about the layout plan that Father gave. Each page is based on a verse from the Word and a declaration arising from it - and those were the ones we used for the declarations when we first started declaring them at TBC.

First I set up the structure of the page, ie the title, arising out of the verse - which I ask the Lord to show me; followed by the verse itself. Leaving a space between I then add the "Blessing Declaration", that goes with the verse; and then I add, for "Further Study", any other verses that may be relevant to our declaration verse and readers may wish to look up for themselves.

Having set up the 'structure' - I then concentrate on the content for the 'space'! I spend time looking at the various translations of the verse in question, followed by the meaning given in various commentaries. And while doing that I ask the Lord to guide my thoughts in the direction He wants to take me. To be honest, it's quite often only one thought initially to kick off with.... then I trust the Lord to show me more, as I start from the point He first gives me.

Actually, it's quite exciting, although pretty challenging at the same time. You see I never really know what's going to end up in that section - until I've finished writing it!

I'd like to share with you that the way Father taught me and helped me to write the content for the Blessing Daily, has been such a tremendous help as I've been writing this book! I can't begin to tell you the number of times I've been completely stuck and not known what I should write.... and then a thought will come, which I start writing with and then gradually the Spirit shows me more. And this has been especially true concerning the detail through the years - I know there's no way I would have been able to share over 70 years of memories without His help!

CHAPTER 9

A Game Changer!

9/1 Exchange Time

How It All Kicked Off!

If I'm honest, I think it all originally kicked off back when the 'tide turned' in 1970.... when, first of all God stepped in and saved my life - and then 'turned the tide' as a result! So what I'm saying is, that all Father's done in my life has followed on from that time. I want to share with you now about the latest 'kick off' - how it started in 2020 just before the pandemic arrived, and has continued since then and, to a degree is still in momentum as I write this!

But, before I launch into that phase of my story - I need to share with you something that happened at High Leigh in the autumn of the previous year. Esther, from TBC came with me for the first time. As you can imagine we knew each other pretty well by this time but, after only having been there for a short time, she said she thought she was seeing the real me there at High Leigh, where I was obviously so much 'at home', for the first time! Thinking about it I realised that I was so relaxed and at home with folk I'd known for many, many years - some even for about 30 years - that it showed... and Esther picked that up. It was only later that I could see that it was more than that!

In February 2020, literally only a week or so before the first lockdown, I went to the Ladies Rise Up weekend - held in a hotel not far from Northampton. For me it was my second time but, this time round, I was able to stay for the whole weekend (the previous year I had to leave after the Saturday night meeting) and leave, like everyone else, after the Sunday morning meeting and lunch. We had a blessed time of praise, prayer, worship and ministry and I believe this helped all of us as we entered the difficult time ahead which, at that point we were totally unaware of as being on it's way..... God is so faithful and loving in the way He prepares us - even when we're mostly unaware of Him doing so!

It was towards the end of the Sunday Morning meeting that the Lord spoke to me, in a totally unexpected way! Clare had been ministering the Word in the meeting, and finished up by sharing how the Lord had dealt with her when younger, over the issue she had concerning 'anxiety and being accepted' by others.... She had placed a 'line' across the front, where she'd been speaking, and encouraged all those who the Lord had spoken to concerning an issue in their lives, whatever it might be, to come forward and 'step over the line'. This would be an 'Exchange' and symbolic of leaving, whatever the Lord had highlighted that needed to go, behind them and to move forward and trust that they had given it to Him and let it go.

When Clare shared what she did, my stomach began to 'churn' and I knew the Lord was digging, challenging and sorting. I knew I had to do something pretty quickly, and get it out in the open or else the enemy would have me tied up in knots over it.... I don't, actually I should say didn't (because He's changed me!) 'spill the beans' to people very easily. But Father was very gracious with me, as the person I spoke to at the front was, and is, a close friend - such a help, as it helped me to vocalise what had taken place! And so I stepped over the line and made the exchange that I needed to.... and will share more of what it was about, as we go on.

It's so wonderful to know that our Father never gives up on us - but always goes on working and changing us into all He has planned and wants us to be. Have you come to that place when you know the truth of this in your heart and life? If you haven't - then now is the time to ask your Father to do whatever needs to be done to accomplish it! Be aware that the enemy will always fight you over it; but remember that our God is greater and has given us the weapons - praise, power, and authority - to fight off whatever he might throw at us - we just have to use them....

What Did I Exchange?

What I 'exchanged' initially was exactly what Clare had shared that she had - the issue of ‘anxiety and being accepted’. I say ‘initially’ because, at that point, I had no idea of all the other things that it kicked off which, to be honest, are still coming up - but the start of it all was the issue over anxiety and being accepted that I ‘exchanged’ and went forward and ‘over the line’ for! And the first thing the Lord brought up to be added to what I’d gone over the line for, as I shared with my friend, was what Esther had said the previous year at High Leigh about seeing the ‘real me’! I began to realise, in a way I never had before, that I needed to acknowledge (along with the anxiety and acceptance issue) - that I was very good at covering up the ‘real me’.....

I have to admit that I felt very wobbly as I went through to lunch afterwards, prior to driving home - and, as I was giving someone a lift most of the way back, wasn’t free to talk it all through with the Lord until I arrived home! I made the 'exchange' not fully understanding what was being dealt with and, actually, it wasn’t till later that night that I understood more of what the Lord had brought up and dealt with in the ‘exchange’ I’d made.... He reminded me of when I was young, right up to the time I was 20 when I first came to know Him - I always found it hard to make friends; always anxious around people and going to places. Also, although I had no doubt of Father’s love for me, I always found it hard to accept that ‘people’ could actually love me. He gradually changed me over the years but it was only with the challenge of the exchange, that I realised how much of that was still buried!

As well as being reminded that evening of details of why the Lord had brought me to that point of making the exchange, I began to realise that actually the ‘exchange’ was just the beginning of the sorting out that Father had started - there was more work still to be done. But even then, I never dreamed or imagined what lay ahead, and that really it was the first step into a new season in my life - with many challenges to be faced in the days, weeks and months ahead!

I trust you've learned, or are learning.... that when Father starts showing us things that need to be dealt with - both as regards to what's going on inside us, or what's going on outside in the way we live our lives; it's because He loves us. And remember there's no force involved - He has given us free will and we have a choice. That's why we're 'human' - not a 'robot'!

When He's dealing with things I have found that, sometimes it's all done in one action, although we still have to live it out in our lives. But at other times, what we might think is the complete action is, in fact, just the beginning - which I began to realise was the case with me, in what happened at Rise Up. I realised it was only the beginning and I knew the three areas in my life that had been pin pointed - anxiety, acceptance and reality. What I didn't know initially was that it was the start of a journey He was taking me on, to dig deep into what was going on inside me and to gradually bring things to the surface and clear them out!

The Start of the Digging

Actually I did come into a certain degree of greater freedom after 'crossing the line' at first - even though I knew there was more to be done! I think the 'start' of the 'digging' came after a phone call from Dawn, Maureen's eldest daughter of the four younger children, on 1 May 2020. She had been notified of the death of Geoff (her father and Maureen's second husband) who was in prison and died of covid. She was also told that he'd had her down as 'next of kin' and this meant that she would be responsible for arranging the funeral. In due course his body would be sent over to the funeral director in Bridgwater.

I never met Geoff, although Maureen had shared with me a fair amount about their lives together, and it's not 'my story' to explain why he was in prison. After a few days I became aware that I was a bit in shock from Dawn's phone call and couldn't work out why initially - as I said, I never knew Geoff, so it wasn't that. Then I began to see that the situation had stirred up all sorts of memories and emotions from the past, and there were things that the Lord was challenging me over that I needed to confront and deal with. Also, with all the limitations re lockdown etc - the enemy had been working hard to start me on the self pity 'track', and feel sorry for myself that Maureen was no longer there to keep me company through it! All lies that had to be dealt with to stop them getting a hold....

One of the things Freda used to say to us, especially when we met up at High Leigh, was that we needed to do our 'homework'! This came back to me several times and so strongly! I really felt the Lord was saying this was the time for me to get my 'homework' done and do the clearing up that was needed - in other words I needed to do the 'processing' bit!!..... On top of that it seemed that pretty well everything I read and heard was about the matter of 'forgiveness' - and the final article I read was by Corrie Ten Boom sharing how the Lord had brought her to a place of forgiving one of her guards from the concentration camp, when she met him years later.

Yes, the first thing that started to surface was the lack of forgiveness in my heart - both inside and outside of the family. Do you remember me sharing with you way back in Chapter 4/2 how the Lord had dealt with me about forgiving the head teacher at the first school I taught at in the East End of London? I shared then about Him doing more in the area of forgiveness at a later date in my life - the 'later date', when it started, was in the May of the year the pandemic arrived, and I will share more as I go further on.....

I shared earlier how the phone call about Geoff's death somehow set off and stirred up all sorts of memories and emotions from the past. Alongside the issue of forgiveness coming to the surface, were a multitude of memories and emotions, particularly in connection with the time when Maureen was terminally ill through the summer of 2014. By 2020 I'd become quite used to writing things down in a journal (will share more in due course about how that came about), and when my friend I shared with regularly, suggested that it might help if I wrote down what was happening, plus what had happened during Maureen's illness - I knew I needed to talk with the Lord about it.

As I shared in Chapter 4/2 concerning finding lack of forgiveness in our heart - it is vitally important to ask the Lord to help us to deal with it. And I'll reiterate what I said then - unless we get it sorted, we're the one who suffers most and are harmed by hanging onto it. It can cause an amazing amount of anger to build up inside and the stress of it all will very often lead to ill health. In the Lord's Prayer it says very clearly about us

forgiving others, as we have been forgiven. I'm not saying it's easy but I do know that Father will give us all the help we need - if we're willing to accept it..... I hope to share more of how He helped me in this area, as things began to surface - some of them, I wasn't even aware of.

The Final 'Push'

The final 'push', as it were, to really start it all moving, came on the evening of 17 May when I sat in bed listening to the worship song "Living Hope". Do you ever find that you can hear or sing something that is actually very familiar, and suddenly find the Holy Spirit is moving in you - highlighting and stirring your spirit and speaking to you in a way you hadn't expected? Well, that's precisely what happened as I joined in worship in that song! It almost seemed as though I'd never heard some of the words and phrases before - especially about the chains being broken and Jesus speaking in the darkness.

I didn't really know what was happening - but I knew the Holy Spirit was doing something in me in connection with all the 'pushing down' re the time I was nursing Maureen and it made me tearful - not something that happened very often! I did realise that it was the real beginning of the 'sorting out' that needed to take place within me.

The following morning I found that there were loads of memories beginning to surface and realised that, part of the sorting, was recognising and forgiving people I was angry at during the time of Maureen's illness. In my journal that morning I noted that I knew there was a long way to go - but I thought it had started!

I've shared with you before about how I believe that the Lord is never in a hurry.... and the process He began to take me through after the exchange I made at Rise Up, highlighted it again! I guess you're beginning to get the picture of just how many different aspects seem to be involved - at least some of them, as there are more to come. After so many years of pushing things down below the surface - it was taking time for the Holy Spirit to bring them up again to the surface in order to deal with them....

It's only as I look back that I'm beginning to realise how gracious the Lord was in the steps He took me along - revealing things to me gradually, and giving me time to take it all in and showing me what I needed to do and why. The fact that it was lockdown played a part as well, because I was able to have more time at home quietly, and start to work it through with the help of the Holy Spirit.

I would encourage you, when you're facing difficulties and you don't really know what's going on, to try and take some 'time out' (if that's at all possible) and just 'sit' with Jesus - and let Him talk to you about it all. Let's face it - He really is the only One who has the answers......

9/2 Time to Sort it Out!

Extra Activity

Alongside everything else that was going on through this time I've been sharing about in the first section of this chapter; there was something else happening that I will attempt to put you in the picture about.... You could say - a different type of 'sorting out'!

I'd been very aware all though my life of the fact that it was very seldom that I cried - although there were times when I would have quite liked to, but nothing really materialised. Looking back through the years, the only time I remember breaking down completely in uncontrollable sobbing, was the night the Lord 'turned the tide' in me - back in August 1970. I'm not saying I never cried, because I did on occasion - particularly when Maureen was so ill and then went to be with the Lord. But, for the most part, it just didn't happen.

In fact there were times, as I went on with the Lord, that I asked Him to soften my heart - I was aware of a certain amount of hardness, some of it I would imagine because I kept quite a tight control on myself, which actually was part of my inability to show the 'real me'! Actually, I remember in particular, being in a meeting on the evening of my birthday and specifically asking Him again to soften my heart - I believe it was the March about a year prior to making the exchange at Rise Up.....

I've shared the back ground in as much detail as I can - so you'll have a greater understanding of what's been happening within me, along with the other changes that have taken place!

As the Lord began to take me forward after the exchange at Rise Up I began to find that, as occasions cropped up that stirred me in my spirit, so there would be some tears coming as well - sometimes just a few, sometimes a lot more.... I began to understand and realise that, as I allowed the Holy Spirit to work in me more and more to sort everything out, so my heart became softer and more responsive to His working.

I would also find that there were occasions when worshipping, that I'd be really moved by the words and content, and feel the tears coming - which was fine when I was on my own, but not something I was completely free in when in a gathering with others! In fact it was in worship at Rise Up two years after I made the exchange, that I experienced the first time I let them actually come in a meeting - and not stop them.....

I'm not going to go into endless examples of my experience in this area of being moved to tears and weeping in the Holy Spirit - but I did feel I needed to share something of what He had done in me. Once again it's a part of being real and open and testifying to Father's power and work in my life - and I know that I have loads more to learn!

As you've probably realised - I've been, and still am, learning a lot in this area concerning being real and open. But I also need to add that we always need to know from the Holy Spirit whether He's the one moving us - and it's not just our emotions getting the upper hand in situations. Our emotions are very real and

also extremely important in the way we live our lives, and are God given - a gift from Father. However, so often we can move in two directions that are not healthy and not of the Lord - instead of functioning in the way He designed us.

It's easy to let our emotions get such a hold on us, that they become the ruling force in our lives. Or else we go the other way, which sadly is what I did, and we push the majority of our emotions down below the surface - very often without realising that's what has happened - and at some stage, often through trauma of some sort, they all decide they want to come to the surface because they've been dealt with inadequately.....In due course I hope to share more about this - a little further on in my story.

My Sabbath Weekend

Do you remember me saying in the first section of this chapter, after I realised so much was being stirred up in me, that I needed to talk to the Lord about the way ahead? Well, the following weekend (23 / 24 May) I set aside some time just to be quiet with the Lord. I have a place in my garden that I call my 'secret place'- and I often sit there with Jesus.... That's what I did that weekend and ended up calling it 'my sabbath weekend', as I did very little else and I felt He planned the time out for me.

I started off just sitting in the sun and praying in tongues for a while, having asked Father to show me what needed to be accomplished and how to go about doing it! Pretty basic I suppose really, but I felt that needed to be the starting point!! Praise the Lord for giving us a heavenly language - so helpful and powerful.

It was while I was praying that I realised that, in fact, there were two avenues at this point that I needed to go down in order to start to sort / clear things out. One was the whole area of 'forgiveness' that I had to address; the other was 'memories' that needed to be processed....

I knew that the 'forgiveness' avenue would be ongoing, even after I'd had the current sort out! The 'memories' might be lengthy but could hopefully be completed as a whole (at least the ones connected with Maureen) - and kept up to date if needed. I would need to persist, but it was possible. I'd thought initially I could just tackle things as they came to the surface, but I realised it would be all too easy to avoid things. The only way actually, was to start from the beginning and write it all down, and that would also highlight those I needed to forgive along the way and be able to deal with that side of things.

I encouraged you, at the end of the first section of this chapter, to take 'time out' with Jesus if you've difficulties in your life - and you're not sure what to do.... I believe it's vital, as we walk with Him - especially so in this busy world we live in, where everything is done at speed and frequently we don't feel we have the time to think things through. If you look at the rhythm of Jesus' life, as portrayed in the Gospels, the authors write often of Him withdrawing on His own to pray. If He needed to do so - how much more should we follow His example!

The 'How?' Of It

I did actually start writing the account - later on that Saturday (23 May) - and called it "My Journey through Cancer with

Maureen". I knew it wasn't something I should rush, but take it slowly with the Lord helping me - and actually it took about three months, finishing towards the end of August. And then I started on another account (Following On) as I realised I needed to write about the time following - when I found myself living on my own again. But I need to leave it there for the moment - or I'll be getting ahead of myself, and the Lord too.....

I also started out on the 'forgiveness' avenue as well, that weekend.... as the Lord helped and showed me what I should do. I went through with the Lord and made a list of those I was already aware of that I needed to forgive - and trusted that He would show me more, as time went on - especially through the writing. On the Saturday evening I celebrated communion with the Lord - and named before Him all those who I was already aware of - a sort of 'first step' - and stated that I forgave them, asking Him to forgive me for the way I had felt about them. I experienced peace and was confident that He would take me further in due course.

I'm sure you realise 'forgiveness' is far more than just saying 'I forgive' - it takes time.... But to even start that journey we first have to be willing and want to go on it - even when our emotions are more than likely screaming out against it. That's when we have to make a choice - whether to live in our emotions or choose to do what we believe the Lord is showing us to do. And be aware, that in making that first step you probably won't feel any differently about the situation - and will still have all the 'anti' emotions about it to contend with.

However, in making that choice, we have released it all into the hands of the Holy Spirit - we're no longer in it on our own.

Praise the Lord!! We will have the help of the Holy Spirit and the grace of God as we move forward - no matter how long it is until our emotions catch up with our choice.

And there's another challenge involved - we need to pray for the person the Lord has shown we need to forgive. That isn't easy either! But there will come a time when you suddenly realise that something's changed - and you realise that you really have forgiven and especially are aware that the 'anger' is no longer there. God is so good and so gracious with us. Thank You Lord!

More Insight re the Memories

It was at Geoff's funeral, which took place at the crematorium on 26 May (the Tuesday after my 'sabbath weekend'), when the Lord gave me a greater insight into the 'memories' situation. Dawn had made all the arrangements concerning her father, with the lady who took the funeral. But she also asked her to give a short memorial to her Mum, Maureen, at the end. This came about because Maureen had chosen, for various reasons, not to have a funeral - and I had carried out her request, which also included a family get together for a celebratory meal about three weeks after she had gone to be with the Lord.

It was when the lady was giving the memorial for Maureen, giving thanks for her life, that I found myself feeling quite 'wobbly' inside. And this increased greatly when a song Dawn had chosen, one of her Mum's favourites, was played. Dawn had chosen Marilyn Baker's song: "Rest in His love, relax in His care....Jesus is here...." and I found myself getting even more wobbly and welling up with tears. Definitely not what I wanted to do in front of everybody!

When I was sitting thinking it through and talking with the Lord about it the following afternoon, I had to admit that I was a bit surprised at just how stirred up I'd been. I suppose I was prepared in my head but not really in my emotions and heart and it highlighted to me just how much 'pushing down' I'd managed to do.

I think it was probably at that point, that I began to realise to what extent I'd pushed so much down out of the way, instead of facing and dealing with it! In fact I had to start to acknowledge that I had never grieved properly for Maureen - just pushed it all down out of the way.... getting through it by God's grace through praise and worship. When I shared with my friend the fact that I'd realised I'd never really allowed myself to grieve properly - she said she had wondered if that was the case. And she encouraged me that the Lord was now in the process of healing and restoring me in what He was leading me through.

I don't know about you, but I know I've been very good through my life at pushing things down below the surface and not acknowledging or dealing with them - as you've probably realised by now! However, I also believe that if we're really serious about going forward in our relationship with the Lord - He'll find a way, no matter how long it might take, to bring us to the place where we'll allow Him to sort us out. His love and patience is so great that He'll go to any length needed to accomplish it - and I am so thankful for the way He has done, and to be honest is still doing, this in my life.....

God Challenged Me

I feel I need to share with you a situation the Lord used to illustrate some of the things He was doing in me at this time - which I found very challenging.... It happened on the Thursday, immediately after Geoff's funeral had stirred things up in me.

You see, I'd shared with my friend and with Joe, Josie and Esther (TBC) about the funeral and asked them to pray - but I hadn't shared any of it with the folk at BCC, in spite of the fact that some of them knew Maureen and some of the members of the family.... On the afternoon after the day of the funeral, when I realised I had never grieved properly for Maureen - the Lord also convicted me of the fact that I should have shared it. In fact, at our BCC zoom meeting in the evening, when asked if I'd had a good day - I'm ashamed to say I'd just grinned and said "Yes, I have" - which really was inexcusable in the circumstances.....

At that point, after I'd been convicted about it, I thought up the idea of sending an email to folk explaining it all. However.... when I woke early the next morning, feeling sick in the pit of my stomach, I knew that wasn't any good. I'm so stubborn at times which is so stupid, I really didn't want anything to hinder my walk with Jesus - so later that day I let Colin know that I wanted to share something when we met again on zoom that evening. Immediately I'd come into agreement with the Holy Spirit - the peace came.

That night I reminded them of a Sunday morning meeting sometime previously, when we had talked about the need to be honest with one another. I explained about Geoff's death and the funeral in Maureen's family and shared with them how the Lord had convicted me about the fact that I hadn't asked them to pray about the funeral etc; and how I had said that I'd had a 'good day' on the Tuesday - which was totally incorrect.

I shared this with you, not just because I found it so challenging (which I did), but because I realised 'why' I needed to go through it. You see I believe that the Lord highlighted to me, in a very practical way, how essential it is to be honest with those we're walking with in the Body - but at the core of it was the need to 'be real' in all things in our lives and with all those we are in contact with.....

I'm not saying we need to share everything with 'all and sundry' but I do believe we need to be real and honest with those we are walking in fellowship with. And we also need those, that we know to be a 'safe place', who we are able to share the deeply personal things in our lives with. Yes, we share and acknowledge them with the Lord, but sometimes they need to be brought out into the open and acknowledged before another person - it 'beds' them, into our spirit and it doesn't give the enemy such opportunity to chase us around on them!

Where to Now?

Having shared fairly comprehensively about what happened in the months following the exchange I made at Rise Up just before the pandemic started, I want to try and give you an idea of how the Lord built on that - and continued to take me forward. But let me just say, what He took me through during that time, was really the start of a new season and an 'Adventure' that He continues to be travelling with me on. Praise the Lord!

It had been a bit of a bumpy ride in places, and continues to be, but the assurance that Jesus was with me through it all made such a difference. That, and knowing that He loves me enough to take the trouble to sort out what's needed in me - to make it possible to go deeper with Him.... All worth it.....

9/3 Going Deeper

The Next Step Forward

I continued to work through with the Lord what He'd been highlighting in my life that needed sorting. As we moved into the second half of the year, and were still very restricted in what we were able to do - I took the opportunity to read more, as well as continuing to write about what I had been through with Maureen, and the time following. And I continued to produce the declarations and post them.... along with working on the Blessing Daily.

I had a growing realisation that I wanted to go deeper in my love relationship with Jesus - which, at the same time, made me aware that there was so much more in me that needed to change to be able to bring that about! A friend recommended a book to me that she had found helpful but extremely challenging! The book has the title: "Emotionally Healthy Spirituality" by Peter Scazzero; and on the cover it says....'It's impossible to be spiritually mature while remaining emotionally immature'.

I want to share a little with you about setting out on this journey, which I feel is the best way to describe it. It won't be possible to go into great detail of my journey, in the parameters of this book. However, I will endeavour to share some of the impact it has had, and to be honest, continues to have as I walk further on with Jesus, and I would recommend the book to you if you're in a place where you desire to walk deeper.

I want to encourage you to remember that our Father never sets us up for impossible tasks that we are not able to accomplish - although we might think at times that there's no way that we can! And, actually, in some ways we're right in thinking that we can't - but - and it's a big BUT - if that's what we're being faced with, the Holy Spirit is in us to help us and bring us through the challenges put before us. He will prepare us and lead us forward one step at a time....

I knew that He had helped me through all the challenging months of sorting out through 2020; and would continue to as I embarked, at the end of the year, on the journey ahead through both the EHS and the Day by Day books. And I will share more about the Day by Day book when we come to it.

Walking Deeper

I embarked on the journey through the EHS book at the very end of 2020 - 30th December and immediately was challenged with this comment, that seemed to jump out at me: "Sometimes 'pretending' can feel safer than honesty and vulnerability!" It struck a chord - I have to be honest.... And the next was concerning the need that "...the way I live my Christian life" needed "...to transform the deep places in my life...". Don't worry, I'm not about to inundate you with quotations from the book! I just want to 'set the scene' as I start to share with you some of the journey I embarked on.

Added to this was the Word the Lord gave me going in to the New Year of 2021 - DEEPER. And along with this was verse 10 of Psalm 25 (Living Bible) - "....when we obey him, every path he guides us on is fragrant with his loving-kindness and his truth." A verse actually, that the Lord gave to me in my early years at Daventry, way back at the beginning of the '70's - and which has always been such a help to me....

Near the beginning of the second section of this chapter I shared a bit about how we can tend to push our emotions beneath the surface - which means we don't really deal with them. I said I wanted to share more on this in due course and hope to do so as I share something of how the Lord worked with me through the 'EHS' book, as I tend to call it - which was more a study and learning manual, than just a book I was reading....

When I tell you that it took me six months to work my way through the book - you'll realise that I took it slowly and really looked to the Lord to help me to understand what He wanted me to. I would read through part of a chapter and underline anything that my spirit particularly responded to (I have never been in the habit of marking books but felt it was necessary this time!). Then I would go through it again and write notes on the section I'd read and anything I felt the Holy Spirit was putting His finger on; and asked Him to show me how to deal with anything that needed to be dealt with. At the end of each chapter there was a prayer highlighting a particular aspect, which the author strongly advised we should pray in connection with our own lives.

I think this was a 'first' for me inasmuch that I'd never been a person to really think and examine what was going on inside of me; much less formulate an answer! This had begun to change rapidly after making the 'exchange' at Rise Up and, as I worked through the EHS book, I found that I was venturing even deeper

through all the challenges I was being faced with. But I found that instead of pushing things down out of sight - I was facing them and, with the help of the Holy Spirit, trying to answer them honestly.....

My Response to the EHS Book

As I gradually worked my way through each chapter I became aware that there was more 'digging' going on - just as effective as that of the digging in the early / mid part of the previous year, but different in the way it was happening. As I write this and look back it makes me think of the digging that takes place in the garden, when the soil is turned over ready for planting and all the weeds are taken out in order not to hinder the growth of the new seeds being planted!

Some of it was very emotional, as things were stirred deeply within me and I was confronted with dealing with them - and there were many tears, but with them the knowledge that my heart was being softened and my emotions being brought more in line to how my Father had created me. I knew, just from the fact that this was happening, that there was a lot going on and that I was learning more about not having a tight hold on my emotions! It felt as though my inner life was being brought into a more orderly form to enable me to go forward in this 'adventure' that I was on and would help me to be able to take part in God's plan for me.

Actually, I believe it built on what I'd already begun to learn through all that had been happening since the exchange and gave me the courage to look 'inside' at what was going on, be willing to deal with anything that was needed and to change going forward.

And it made me more willing to bring things out into the open and acknowledge them as part of dealing with them, rather than just pushing them down out of the way.

Once again I was so aware of Father's timing in it all and fully aware that, if I'd been going through it any time prior to this, I just wouldn't have had the level of understanding that I needed to have. It thrilled me to know that He had already been 'digging' over the ground and had begun to remove weeds in preparation.

Remember, and I know I've said this before..... 'Nothing' that happens in our lives is never, ever wasted.....

More Lessons Learned

As I continued on my journey through the book, I began to understand more about the need of having a balanced and stable emotional life that reflected the way that Jesus lived His life when He lived amongst us. And the importance of this, if we wanted to be in a place where we could help those that Father brought into our lives.

But, I also began to understand, that this actually, was really only 'one side of the coin'..... What we also needed, walking in harmony with this, was a balanced spiritual life. The author of the book referred to it as 'rhythms of life' - the need to be in a daily rhythm in our walk with Jesus and it was the cohesiveness / combination of both that gave the balance that was healthy.

I certainly began to realise, more than I had ever done before, that none of this happens 'overnight'! It all needs working at -

but not in the way of working and making it happen through our own efforts..... that's not what I'm saying. Jesus has already done it all for us on the cross, praise the Lord! But the 'working at it' is our being willing to let the Holy Spirit lead us and teach us all we need to know - and this will probably not be complete, until we are taken home to glory.

Day by Day Book

This is a 40 day devotional that links in with the EHS book and is written by its author to guide and help those who want to go further and deeper with Jesus. The '40 days' are actually 8 weeks which work with the content of the eight chapters of the EHS book. The aim is to help those who want to have regular times with the Lord each day, that are really meaningful and not just 'compulsory sessions'. Many people find they have a tendency to talk to God, or possibly 'at' God - but seem unable to actually listen to Him; or to just spend time with Him because they love Him!

Some of the problem being is that their lives rush along at such a pace - it seems difficult to take time out with God that is meaningful. Their 'God time' is squeezed in at some point, fitting in with everything else going on in their lives - often because they feel they should, not necessarily because they want to..... Whereas it should be the opposite. Our 'God time' should be central - with the rest of our lives arranged around it - and with His grace and help that is possible.

Let me hasten to say that I'm not saying that the way it's done in this book is the way we should all be following - far from it.

But, having worked through it (actually something I have now done twice, with quite a gap between) what I learned from it I have found invaluable in the way I've formed new patterns of spending time with Jesus through each day and, in many ways, new content also..... Not to mention the place the Lord has brought me to in being able to face the challenges that I've needed to face in order to grow in my love relationship with Him.

Every one of us are uniquely created by our loving Father - so it follows that each one of us, with His help, need to discover and follow the path He shows us in relation to 'how, when and where' we spend regular time with Him! What I will say is that the whole pattern of my walk and daily time spent with Him has been somewhat revolutionised and has definitely been deepened. For more years than I can remember I've talked with Jesus throughout the day (and often at night as well) - about everything going on in my life and around me - and that hasn't changed. But the 'specific' times I spend with Him through the day, and the pattern of them, has changed.....

CHAPTER 10

My Journey with Jesus

10/1 My Writing Story

Have I Always Wanted to Write?

Before I go any further in this final chapter, I'd like to share with you more about my writing 'story'! I've shared a fair amount on the way through to here already - mainly as to how I came to be actually writing this book. But, what I haven't really said much about is, how the Lord has given me the ability to do so. You see, in answer to the above question: "Have I Always Wanted to Write?" - it has to be a definite "No!"..... a big part being, that I didn't think I was actually capable of being able to.

Back in November of 2020 the Lord spoke to me about needing to record my 'writing story'. To say it was rather a shock, is something of an understatement - I wasn't even aware that I had one to share, which is why it was such a shock! At the time I did share with a friend - I knew I'd more than likely bury it, if I didn't acknowledge it.... I did bits here and there but it wasn't until the following February that I really did anything about actually completing it, and shared it with my friend.

I hope you'll understand more, as you read what the Lord gave me to share - why I was so surprised at what He had said to me. I really didn't understand the background of it all, until I began to be obedient and started to write it as He'd told me to. It was such a lesson to me again of Him guiding and working in my life, literally for many years, when I really hadn't got a clue as to where it was heading. But - when I'd written it, I had such a sense of excitement to realise He'd been leading me in the direction of writing - pretty well for most of my life. How incredible and encouraging is that!

The Early Years

When I was in school I don't really remember anything particularly startling about my English lessons and writing anything creatively; or, for that matter, in any of my other subjects. If anything, what I remember more, is the difficulty I often found in putting anything on paper that expressed what I wanted to say! And I definitely never attempted to write anything personal concerning how I felt about myself or my feelings.....

Once I was at college, about four years later and starting my teacher training, I was once again in the situation of having to express myself on paper..... I was training to be a

Junior/Secondary teacher, which covered the children in the top classes of the junior school as well as those in the secondary school who were aged 11 years upwards. This meant I needed to have the basic knowledge of the range of subjects taught to primary school children, as well as the specialist subjects I was following to teach the secondary age group. These were Divinity as my main, and Geography, as my secondary subject.

English was one of our 'core' subjects and not optional - otherwise I would probably have opted out! The main thing that I remember about the English course I did at college was that, on one of the long summer breaks, we had to produce the first chapter of a book that we might like to write. How horrific! Was my first thought.... I remember that, because I'd read the Narnia stories since I'd started my college course in the autumn of 1986, I decided that somehow my 'first chapter' would be from another book in the series. I think it's the only time I ever remember writing anything creatively and, the amazing thing was, that my English tutor actually complimented me on it!

My memory through the years is of always finding it difficult to put things into words on paper and, when I did, it was as brief as possible because it was such hard work. I never particularly wanted to keep any sort of a diary or journal, as I could never think what to put into it! In fact, I always used to wonder at how people could produce enough every day, to keep a diary.....

One thing that has come back to me as I've been sharing this with you is, that I've remembered that whenever I did find I had to write anything - I would make sure it was as short as possible. In other words - I'd only put on paper the least number of words

to express what I had to - and no more..... Nowadays, I start writing and it just seems to keep on flowing - and then I suddenly realise and 'laugh' with Jesus and thank Him for what He's done in me. Did you know that you can laugh with Jesus?

As I Grew Older

I don't remember writing very much at all as I got older, although I think I did write a fair amount in my letters to my friend Jenny - when she was away in New Zealand for six months. And then again when she was in the States, which I think was for about four months. Actually, thinking about it now, I believe I wrote a fair amount home when I was in Iran. I had to in a way, particularly to those churches who were supporting me through the Church Missionary Society who had sent me out there.... And I also wrote a fair amount to Peter and Jean.

Again - I realise now it was all part of the training and preparation for a later season. Remember, Father is never in a hurry and never wastes anything that He allows to happen in our lives. It's so reassuring to be reminded again that He leads us on - one step at a time.

A New Season

I think it was after Maureen had gone to be with the Lord, and I was with Joe and Josie in the church they were planting in Bridgwater, that things began to move re the writing.... This was particularly so as I began to work on the administration side of things, as we became a registered charity, and I became a trustee as well. I have shared this more fully in Chapter 8, where I also explained how I became involved in, and eventually became responsible, for the Declarations. And how this led on to starting work on The Blessing Daily (Vol 1) as well.

But, as I also shared in Chapter 8, as well as being involved in writing and putting together the 'Daily' - I was also involved in writing this book "The Turning of the Tide"..... the start of which was initially highlighted and alerted by the Holy Spirit in May 2016. It was a very slow beginning, possibly because I was pretty tied up with everything else going on at TBC; possibly because I hadn't really acknowledged it openly to anyone - not even to Joe who'd been the one the Lord used to speak to me!

It wasn't really until into 2020 that I began writing my own book in earnest, and especially so after I'd shared with Joe what I was doing. He offered his help, which I greatly appreciated, and I was also able to share how the Lord had used him in the years we worked together in TBC in Bridgwater (and continues to) to draw out from me the ability to write. I can't emphasise enough the fact that I really didn't know that I possessed the ability to write and, even more than that - I never had the desire to.

Alongside that was the encouragement my friend gave me to write about the journey I went on when my friend Maureen was ill, and afterwards also - which the Lord used to help me to finally grieve properly, instead of just pushing it down. I believe that in writing that, He taught me how to express what I was feeling in words - and this has helped me so much in writing this book and being honest in all that has happened since the 'exchange' took place at Rise Up in February 2020.

This time was certainly a 'new season' for me in so many ways as I adjusted to living on my own once more and, in many ways, my life was turned around completely as the Lord took me into a new fellowship - a new part of His family. And such a privilege to be part of all He was doing at TBC - but also what He did in my life through it - especially in the steps He took me through in starting to prepare me for the writing that He's given to me to do now.....

Writing Full Time

It was in September of 2021 that I found myself sitting in my 'secret place' in the garden, asking the Lord a very similar question to the one I'd asked Him in May 2020 - about the next step I should take..... Previously I'd been asking the Lord the way ahead in regard to the grieving of Maureen, etc. This time I was asking Him about my way forward concerning Grace Advocacy, the Daily and 'writing' in general..... I'd been gradually feeling less peaceful in the layout and expenditure of my time - sensing there needed to be some changes. For a long time I'd had the desire to be able to spend more time both on the Daily and on the book - but hadn't really felt that the time was right...

It didn't happen overnight but, over a period of time, I began to cut back on the amount that I was doing. Within Grace Advocacy I switched from being involved working with clients on applications for benefits such as PIP, Attendance Allowance, etc; plus any of their debt problems - and worked more on the pastoral side of things and sharing prayer requests. There were a few folk I continued with, but on the whole others took on the responsibility.

Through the pandemic I obviously hadn't been able to go 'out and about' so much - and, basically, I didn't resume again as regulations were eased off. So.... I gradually arrived at the point of spending the majority of my time at home writing - either working on the Blessing Daily or writing this book that you have been reading!

I'm also aware that there is more writing ahead, after the completion of this book! I'd already felt there was more to come and believed the Lord had begun pointing me in the direction of other subjects to tackle - and then I was asked a direct question as to whether I'd had anything from the Lord about writing something on a particular subject they mentioned..... which sort of sealed it for me.

This, in many ways, was a somewhat strange time, when the Lord continued to speak and deal with me about various things going on 'inside' me - but, at the same time, I began to feel I was being pulled in two directions concerning what I was doing. I really wanted to be able to spend more time writing - but part of me wanted to go on helping people through Grace Advocacy!

However, I came to realise again that often we have to be willing to 'let go' - before we can reach out to grasp the new thing that Father has planned for us. I couldn't move into the new season that was ahead - unless I moved out of the season I had been in previously.

10/2 My Journey

Sharing My Journey

Well, dear friends - at least, I hope I can call you friends, as you've stuck with me as far as this.... Thank you for coming on this 'journey' with me and I pray that each one of you have learned more about your own journey with Jesus! I know that I have certainly learned more about mine as I've been writing this....

I never realised that, as I endeavoured to share with you about the years that I have walked through with Jesus - that I would learn so much more about all that Father has done for me during that time. And alongside that I've also learned and, certainly understand so much more, about what He has done 'in' me. I am reminded how, at one point when I was a bit hesitant about sharing certain things that had been painful at the time they happened, my friend, who I'd asked to pray as I began to write about them, pointed out to me "...you're a completely different person to who you were at that time - so it shouldn't affect you...". Praise the Lord - she was absolutely right! The Lord has changed so much within me, that it didn't affect me - and I'm so thankful to Him for demonstrating that to me in the way that He did. And so thankful to Him also for providing me with a friend who walks closely with Him, who could speak into my life in that way....

I do thank the Lord for those in the Body of Christ that He has given me to walk with through the years. Some of them may have only been for a short season; some have been for several seasons over many, many years - and some I continue to walk with as I write this..... all of them very much appreciated. I know that without the input from some of them, that I wouldn't be in the place I'm in now in my relationship with Jesus. And I don't think I'd be doing what I'm doing now either! God is so, so good - and I'm so grateful that He plans in love, for each and every one of us.

As you go forward with the Lord - I want to encourage you to also look back..... I'm not suggesting you look back in an unhealthy way, dwelling on all the hard times and the difficulties you've faced - that's only a sure recipe to start drifting into the realm of self-pity - and the enemy would love to help you all he can in that area! But look back at where you have come from in your walk with Jesus - and all the challenges He has brought you through. You'll be looking at those times in your life when you grew in your love relationship with Him and grew stronger in your walk with Him. You see it's when He brings us through all those difficulties and the challenges they present - that's the very time He helps us to grow......

My Older Years

As you have probably realised by now, my journey with Jesus has covered many years! You may remember me sharing that I made my initial contact and commitment to Jesus when I belonged to the Junos at the age of seven. The seed planted then, didn't actually germinate into a proper commitment of my life until I was aged 21, in the year 1965. As I write this, it's the year 2022 - which makes me 78 years old, and I've been walking with Jesus for 57 years - which I find amazing and humbling all mixed up together!

I want to encourage those of you reading this book who might be in the older age bracket and consider yourself a 'wrinkly' - not to think of yourself as old and no longer of any use to the Lord. I chatted recently with a lady, just into her sixties, who viewed her life as pretty well over and of no further use in the Kingdom. I believe in the course of our conversation, the Holy Spirit was able to turn her thinking around and change her 'mindset' - giving her a different outlook on her life.

I have to own up to having Caleb as my 'pin up' - the only man, other than Joshua, who came out of slavery in Egypt and then, after 40 years in the desert, eventually entered into the Promised Land, given by God to the Israelites. He was 85 years of age by then, but had no hesitation at carrying out the task that his Father had planned for him - and he certainly wasn't going to let his age hold him back in any way whatsoever.....

As I've heard Joyce Meyer often say, "age is only a number", and she knows what she's talking about - she continues in her worldwide ministry at the age of 78 - with her husband Dave, who's 80! Yes, our bodies may slow down a bit as our years advance, and there may be other issues to face.... but it's God that directs our steps and the One who decides when it's time to go home to be with Him. And, quite frankly, until that time comes, I for one, want to be available to be used by Him in helping to build up His Kingdom.

I have to be honest, I don't think 'retirement' actually comes into the equation! Obviously, on the world stage, if we're working in a job we more than likely have to retire. But I don't see that as the case when we walk with the Lord. And as I look

back over the last sixteen years, since I retired from my job, I often think to myself - "How on earth did I find time to work?".....

Lessons Learned - Some of the 'Biggies'....

Don't worry, I'm not going to go through listing and repeating what I've learned through the years! I think I would probably find it harder to do - than you would find ploughing your way through it - plus I can think of nothing worse. But, I would like to share a few of the lessons I learned on my way, as I've walked with Jesus - and am trusting Him to highlight the ones He wants me to - and possibly why..... As far as I'm aware, I've shared them in the context of my story - but feel in my heart to emphasise some of them here.

The first that comes to mind, happened when I was at teacher training college in Salisbury towards the end of the 60's. For the first time, at least it was the first time I registered it, I met up with believers who didn't really seem to have any desire or interest in going on with the Lord. That sounds critical, but I don't mean it to be - although I have to be honest and say I think I was critical at the time. I have to confess that, it's only as I share this now that I've realised and acknowledged that - and have had to pause in my account of it, in order to confess it to the Lord and ask His forgiveness.....

I've often heard it said, that wanting to be a believer, particularly an active one, is 'caught' rather than 'taught' - and I believe it to be true. So, the more the life and love of Jesus can be seen in our lives - the more the people we are with will come to the point where they want what we have! In other words - we need to make them 'hungry' for Jesus.....

I'm sad to say, that I'm not sure there was a great deal about my life back then - to make others hungry. But trust the Lord that it has changed as I've walked deeper with Him through the years.

The issue of living on my own has been one I've faced several times - including once again currently. I think we need to be aware that the enemy will do his level best to upset the apple cart, and try and convince us it's too lonely to live alone. I think the most important thing we need to establish, and we need to go to the Word for the truth of it - is the simple fact that the Word says we will never be alone. The Lord has promised always to be with us! When we ask Him to give us that mind-set to stand on - it changes the whole perspective. It's not something we learn overnight and I have realised, each time I've lived alone, that I actually learn more about going deeper with Jesus through it!

I do believe it's good to share and live together and there's strength in that - but if the Lord gives you a season of living alone, make sure you learn all He wants to teach you!

I have learned that, ultimately, it's 'me and Jesus'! What do I mean by that? I mean that in any given situation - we need to know what Jesus is saying and what He requires us to do.... He needs to be my first 'go to' at all times. I'm not saying not to share with friends and ask them to pray and ask the Lord about it - but crucially we need to know what He wants us to do. Especially when everyone is saying the opposite to what you think He wants.

You have to have a certainty in what you decide to do, if you're going to 'stand your ground' on it. It won't be any good even to attempt to - unless you have that assurance.

It's not an easy situation to go through, and somewhat contradictory, to talk about going through and standing at the same time.... But it's the standing firm and holding fast to what Father has shown you, that brings you through into what He has planned and prepared for you.

We often say 'yes' to doing something and then wish we hadn't! It may not seem much - but I do believe we should carry it out, unless it's completely impossible - for example if we find we're already committed to something else.... We honour the Lord in our walk with Him when we keep and stay true to our word, as it says in Psalms 15:4 "....He who swears to his own hurt and does not change;" The Lord pointed it out to me many years ago - and has reminded me of it on occasions when I've been tempted not to fulfil something I said I would do and not found it easy to either!

Our integrity in our walk with the Lord is vital - and speaks louder than words! What we are in the way we live our lives, speaks of Jesus to all those we are in contact with - and that goes for those who know the Lord and those who don't.... I want to be seen to be honest and dependable in what I do, as well as in what I say. You see, what we say carries no weight whatsoever - if what we do doesn't line up with it. And, if we're not sure what to do in any given situation, if we ask the Holy Spirit - He'll show us!

Learn as much as you can from those the Lord brings you in

contact with throughout your life's journey - but ALWAYS first and foremost keep your eyes focussed on Jesus. Be alert to those you realise are further on in their journey than yourself and who you can see are walking in a deeper love relationship. Spend time with them - and learn more of what it means to be in love with the King of Kings. I often thank the Lord that He brought me in contact in the early years of my walk with Him, with those who helped me lay a foundation to build on. Always have an open heart and spirit to hear what Father is saying to you - especially about the way forward. Learn to listen and understand what He's saying to you and trust Him - He's not going to lead you up a dead end. But at the same time - be sensitive to any warning from the Spirit to hold back when you need to.....

I think really what I'm saying here, and wanting to underline, is that above all the most important thing we need to learn is the importance to keep at the core / centre of our walk with the Lord - is our love relationship with Him. And a vital part of this is being aware of, and listening to the Holy Spirit - and above all being obedient to do what He says to do....

....And the 'Smaller'

I have found through the years, that very often the 'smaller' things the Lord does bless me nearly as much as the 'bigger' things.... Actually, I don't really look on anything He does as being 'small' - all of them, big or small, are ways in which He shows His love for us and are precious. But I'm thinking more of those things that He does for me personally in my day to day life, that wouldn't necessarily mean a lot to others but, to me are precious because the context they occur in, they make a difference. Many of them remain just between Him and me - because, as I said, they mean something to me personally.

For instance, I particularly appreciate Father's help when faced with tasks (of varying difficulty) that I haven't a clue how to do - both in the home and, particularly in connection with doing things online. In fact I believe I shared with you earlier in Chapter 8, how He helped me with things I had to do in connection with the work for the Charity Commission - that I hadn't got a clue about, and no one else in TBC did either. The Holy Spirit is such a great teacher! And I wouldn't be able to count the times I've lost things, especially in the house, and the Lord has shown me where they were - such a relief.

Then there are those times I've not been too sure about something and I've been sent a text or an email, or even received a phone call - and I've found the answer, or the encouragement in them that I've needed. And I've realised that Father has already organised the answer before I needed it and, very often, without me even asking Him.

Just a 'flavour' of how Father looks after us on a day to day basis in our lives. I challenge, and encourage, you to look more closely at those things Father has done in your life - think about them and give Him thanks for the way He loves and looks after you!

Epilogue

The End is in Sight

Wow! The journey through my first book is nearly over - apart from this epilogue! At least the 'writing' part of it is. Of course, there's all the paraphernalia of getting it into print and published to go through yet - not to mention getting it out to people to read.

Praise God that Pastor Joe is on hand to help me - just as he has been to help me all the way through!

Where to Now?

I can't even begin to tell you in words just how amazed I am to have got as far as this with writing this book - it really does blow my mind.... But part of me, is telling the other part of me, that there's no reason to be so knocked over by it all - Father has had it in His hands from the beginning right through to the end and, after all, He is very much the "God of the impossible"!

So..... what am I going to do with myself, when it's completed and out in the market place? If you registered earlier that I referred to it being 'my first book'.... you'll have some idea!

Let me tell you what I do know. I do know that I'm to go on writing - I believe the Lord has made it part of my life. Something I'm to continue with until He tells me otherwise - or takes me home.... And I do have some idea of some of the content of future books. And yes, you read that right - I intentionally put that in the plural.

Now, let me tell you what I don't know! I don't know as yet (at the time of writing) just what my next book will be, but am trusting Father to show me - and also how soon I'm to make a start....

What Has God Shown Me?

What do I know now - that I didn't know prior to writing this book? I know, because I have lived through it, that back at the beginning of 1970 - I felt my life was messed up to such a point that I tried to finish it. I was able to speak the words that said I knew the Lord was able to take care of me and sort things out.... But inside me, in my heart, I have to be honest - I somehow didn't really believe them - otherwise I would not have acted in the way that I did.

BUT when Father stepped in and turned the tide, He began to take me on the 'journey of a lifetime' - a journey that has taken my whole life to travel through. I really do believe that my God is 'God of the impossible' - and He has changed me from the inside out, to bring that about.... and, I believe, is still changing me!

I know now that He will never, ever fail me. I know it's more than likely that He'll do things His way - which always turns out to be the best way. I know that He desires, above anything else, that I walk in a love relationship with Him - and that He has first place in every part of my life. He loves me - and I love Him.

Printed in Great Britain
by Amazon

17915799R20169